The Art of the Tele-Flirt

Flirting in the Digital Age: 77 Mobile, Video, and Texting Ideas You Have to Try

Moni Rogers

The Art of the Tele-Flirt. Flirting in the Digital Age: 77 Mobile, Video, and Texting Ideas You Have to Try

By Moni Rogers

effort has been executed to present accurate, up to date, reliable, complete information. No warranties of any kind are declared or implied. Readers acknowledge that the author is not engaged in rendering legal, financial, medical, or professional advice. The content within this book has been derived from various sources. Please consult a licensed professional before attempting any techniques outlined in this book.

By reading this document, the reader agrees that under no circumstances is the author responsible for any losses, direct or indirect, that are incurred as a result of the use of the information contained within this document, including, but not limited to, errors, omissions, or inaccuracies.

ISBN 978-1-7376687-1-8

Midwest 2 U LLC
Matteson, IL - USA
www.midwest2u.com

Midwest 2 U

Table of Contents

Introduction

First dates are interviews.

—Ryan Reynolds

Modern dating has become digital and has a science of sorts. The world of dating has truly evolved over the ages, and over the past decade or so, dating has entered a new frontier. That frontier is digital and online dating. It has tremendously changed the way the world has viewed dating and has opened a world of opportunities. Some will say for the better, and some will say for the worse. Regardless, online dating is here to stay and is only rising in popularity. Due to the rise of technological advancement, the current COVID-19 pandemic, and the surge of long-distance relationships across the globe, the influence of this dating style has never been more prevalent. It comes with many factors that we need to consider, with reams of dos and don'ts that we need to follow. In addition, dating has become technical and has never been more competitive. We live in an age where we need to stand out from the crowd and brand ourselves as desirable so that we are chosen over and above thousands—nay, millions—of suitors all vying for the attention of their next "one and only."

Due to the complex nature of digital dating, it can be overwhelming. Many people don't know where to even begin. Being single is difficult, and sometimes the search for Mr./Ms. Right can be tough, especially if you are new to this type of dating scene and aren't quite sure of dating etiquette. You need to get an edge on the competition by impressing your match. You also have to learn ways to always keep them wanting more. It is important to navigate through the challenges of the modern dating scene.

In this journey, we will discuss how the world has evolved from dating pre-smartphones to the introduction of the internet and the modern environment of dating as we know it today. We will unpack just how much the internet has changed the world of dating in the past few decades. We will arm you with many strategies and text ideas to always keep the conversation with your match/partner interesting. You will learn a flurry of different techniques and ideas you can try out on your next online conversation so that you will never be left scrambling for words and wondering what to say next.

Next up, we will explore what and what not to do with your dating profile pictures. We will highlight exactly what must be done when selecting the perfect profile pictures to upload on your dating profiles. If you follow these tips, you are sure to see a spike in your match success rate.

Crafting the perfect video date is another thing you need to know. Learn key secrets to ensure a smooth transition of your conversation with your match/partner from text to video. Video dates are important not only for digital and online dating matches but also for people in long-term relationships who want to connect despite the geographic restrictions. Explore some great strategies and tips to ensure that your video date will be a roaring success and lead to further video dates down the line while also reducing the risk of engaging in an awkward video date. On top of that, we have also included fun and creative ideas that you and your match or long-distance partner can do together for an awesome digital date.

Dating apps have popped up everywhere, and sometimes, we are spoiled for choice and can feel a little overwhelmed. That is why we have highlighted a variety of different apps for you to check out. We have pointed out which apps are best suited for you as a person based on your preferences. One suggestion is to find one or two apps that align with your preference and attract the kind of people you are looking for to garner the best results for finding the one. Last but not least, enjoy the 10 commandments of digital and online dating. Treat these commandments as your ultimate guide in this world and follow them at all times.

Once you have garnered the knowledge in this book, we are confident that your search for love will become a lot easier. You will be armed with various digital tactics, techniques, strategies, and tips that will help you master this dating game. We are certain that, if put into action, you will have loads of matches waiting in line to connect with you. The secrets of success for dating on the internet lie within these pages. It is now up to you to put them to good use to find the one.

About the Author

Moni Rogers has developed a no-nonsense suggestion that, if followed correctly, the user will see their dating game hit new peaks of success like never before. Moni Rogers isn't a dating guru or an expert. After Moni suffered a stroke at the age of 29, she had a new outlook on life. She then has years of success in helping people find love and cultivating loving relationships through both digital and physical means. Moni understands human interactions. Moni is incredibly passionate about the world, helping people find love. She finds deep satisfaction in helping people navigate their way through the world of dating, culture, tech, and just living.

Chapter 1:
What Dating Was Like Pre-Smartphones/Internet and How It Has Evolved

Dating through the ages has evolved, taking on many shapes and forms as time progresses from generation to generation. The age of digital and online dating is still a relatively new introduction in the world of dating, and it is constantly evolving as we speak. However, there was a time when dating was purely offline and the age of finding Mr./Ms. Right on our phones, tablets, or laptop screens was never an option. The world never used to be as interconnected as it is today. Back in the day, you were exposed only to people around your vicinity and areas where you resided, worked, or played, and that was that. That all changed with the introduction of the internet, which connected cities, countries, and even continents through a digital web. The internet connected people no matter where they were in the world. This was revolutionary, as the pool for potential matches and love interests skyrocketed! We were no longer dealing with people within a 20-kilometer or a 5-mile radius but instead a radius that knew no limits. It didn't matter anymore, even if you lived in the United States and your match lived in Germany or Australia. A potential romantic connection could form thanks to the power of the internet and advancing digital technologies. For the first time in history, having a love interest thousands of kilometers or miles away from where you lived became feasible.

Old-Fashioned Dating

Dating wasn't always about dating profiles and swiping right on a profile if it piqued your interest or swiping left on a profile if it didn't. The world of dating before the internet was much more complex and oftentimes required more research and elbow grease to ensure you stood out from the crowd (also something called in-person verbal communication). You must understand that 20 to 30 years ago, there were no phones that neatly connected the world together, and if there were phones, they were very basic with very limited functions. There was very little texting and certainly no social media or dating platforms to help you find a potential partner. The age of dating before the internet was tough and very different from how it is set up today.

Dating Before Cell Phones

In the modern era, owning the latest cell phone is all the rage. Whenever Apple or Samsung releases their latest cell phone model, millions of superfans across the globe camp outside cell phone stores, eagerly awaiting to get their hands on the newest model. The scary part is that only after a week of owning the latest model, these super fans of their beloved cell phone brands cannot imagine life without their new device. However, we must remember there was a world before cell phones, and the world was set up very differently because of it, particularly the world of dating. The smartphone-free dating world was very different, and it is a scenario that many older millennials and generations that pre-date millennials would know all too well.

Before the age of smartphones and texting, people looking to find a potential love interest were forced to source telephone/cell phone number after number. It seems quite bizarre in the modern age as it just seems like such an outdated system. Today, nobody scurries around trying to collect digits from various suitors as it is simply old-fashioned and not how it is done in the modern dating world. Today, it's a 50/50 chance you are going to meet your potential boyfriend/girlfriend online on one of the various dating apps, other social media, gaming, or digital tech. Regardless of which avenue you went down, it is unlikely you would ask somebody you are attracted to for their actual cell phone number (Goldfarb, 2014).

However, before dating apps, social media, or even cell phones, you had to get somebody's phone number if you ever actually wanted to see someone again or set another date. What would generally happen is they would write down their ten-digit phone number on a scrap piece of paper, a hand, or a hat, so you always have to carry around a pen. Once you had written their number on, say, a scrap paper, you better be damn sure you protected it with your life and didn't misplace it. If you lost that scrap piece of paper, you lost your only source of contact with your potential mate as you could not just pop the number in your phone, seeing you didn't own a phone. However, if you lost the sacred scrap piece of paper with your potential suitor's number on it, there was a plan B. Plan B, though, was by no means foolproof, as it revolves around looking up your potential match's number in the phone book and praying that their number is listed there. And even if it was listed in the phonebook, it may be outdated.

Giving your crush a call on their landline was the thing back in the day. You must understand that unlike a cell phone, which is used by one person, a landline was used by a household. Thus, calling a landline was always like a game of roulette when it came to who would answer the phone. Occasionally, you would get lucky, and the person you were trying to call would pick up the phone. However, more often than not, your call would be answered by a nosy roommate or, even worse, nosy parents/siblings. So often, you would awkwardly have to mumble on the phone, "Hello, Mrs. Crane, can I please speak to Sarah?" Then if you were lucky, you would finally get hold of Sarah, but that didn't mean somebody wasn't listening in on your conversation on the other line as you asked her if she remembered you from the bus stop and if she would like to go get dinner with you on Friday night (Goldfarb, 2014).

Moreover, there was always the possibility that your boyfriend/girlfriend or a potential match that you were anxiously trying to get hold of wasn't even home. In that case, you would be met with the answering machine, where you would be forced to leave a message, hoping that the person you were trying to reach would get the message. Of course, there was a chance that somebody might just delete the message you left for them.

After managing to reach your crush and successfully setting up a date, you would then have to meet them in person. Anxiety, nerves, and sometimes, frustration would arise when planning the perfect first date. There was no casual "Hey, do you wanna meet up with me tonight?" which you'd sent on the day, expecting them to be available and ready to meet you. No, that wasn't how it went down. When you set up a date with someone before cell phones, you had to have an exact time and exact location, and if someone was running late, there wasn't much you could do other than stay in the specific spot that you two had arranged to meet at. There was no way to quickly say you were running late or you burst a tire; thus, you had to wait and pray they would show up and stay true to their word. Sometimes you would have to wait for hours, unsure of when or if your date was even going to pitch up. However, more often than not, your date would arrive, and assuming that went well, you would now have to maintain the relationship, which was a challenge of its own.

Maintaining a relationship before smartphones were introduced was not easy, and looking back, it seems bewildering how we as humans managed to keep relationships going without the aid of cell phones.

When couples were apart from each other, there was no way to check in with each other throughout the day. Thus, you could not send a "How was your day?" or "Thinking of your message" to your boyfriend or girlfriend. Back then, you kind of just had to wonder how your partner was doing and ignore any lonely or paranoid thoughts your mind may be thinking (Goldfarb, 2014). There were many complications regarding the dating world before cell phones, and dating was not as smooth as it is today in terms of planning dates and communicating with each other. This is something we often take for granted in the smartphone age of dating.

Friends Setting Up Friends

Before apps like Tinder, Bumble, Grindr, or OkCupid, friends used to act as the matchmaker for their friends. Granted, today's friends still help out their friends and still arrange dates for each other, but it is far less common. Today many young singles will rely on the algorithms of dating websites to find a match. However, before the age of dating apps and cell phones, one of the most common ways to meet a love interest was through a friend setting you up. Sometimes, these are blind dates—meaning that you had no idea who you were being set up with and you didn't even know what your date looked like. On a blind date, you just had to trust your friend's intuition. However, these dates set by a friend were not always blind dates. More often than not, you would have seen, heard, or known of the person your friend was setting you up with.

The people whom you spend most of your free time with are your friends, and as such, it is no surprise that you would value their opinions highly. Thus, it was only logical that being set up with a mutual friend was a very popular way to meet your boyfriend, girlfriend, or spouse. Your friends know you. They know what you like and what you dislike. Thus, they are the perfect people to be able to set you up with somebody with like-minded interests and characteristics. Back in the day, your friends were your Tinder.

Moreover, how a couple communicated with each other before cell phones were invented was different from today. Before smartphones, interactions were almost exclusively through face-to-face communication with the odd phone call here and there. It was a different world pre-smartphones, and there was no such thing as couples texting each other back and forth, where you could plan what you were going to say before you sent a text. That simply wasn't the case, as communication was done face-to-face or talking directly over the telephone. Thus, whatever you said was said, and there were no take-backs. What this means is that you have no chance to erase what you already said. It is not like a text, where you can think very carefully about what you want to say and even retype the message if you want to say something different from what you were originally thinking (Jarret, 2016).

What People Miss from Old-Fashioned Dating

Dating before the introduction of the internet, cell phones, and other digital and online platforms wasn't all bad, and like anything, it had its pros and cons.

While we have highlighted the challenges and complexities of dating back in the day, there are aspects of pre-digital and online dating that people miss.

There's no denying that dating has changed through the ages and that most interactions between couples in the 21st century are done digitally. This has changed the dating scene forever. Some will say for the better, and some won't be so quick to agree. One of the major bummers of digital dating today is that couples have lost that sentimentality and that element of romance that many couples of the past put so much effort into. As a 21st-century couple, ask yourself this: "What stuff do you still have from your past lovers?" (Goldfarb, 2013). The answer to that question is most likely a few emoji-riddled texts and a few photos on Instagram, if you're lucky. If you think about what dating looked like for your grandparents or even your parents, they had boxes of love letters stashed in their cupboards. Your grandmother might even have a super romantic love letter your grandfather sent her when he was stationed somewhere in the army. What little trinkets do you have stashed in your cupboard from your lover? Maybe you have a ticket stub to a Knicks game or some photo strip you guys got at a photo booth at one of your cousins' weddings where you both probably drank a little too much. However, how many non-digital photos do you guys have together? The truth is, these very rare non-digital trinkets are important to show your love to your partner off-screen. Wouldn't it be nice to have a physical photo album that the two of you could page through that neatly documents your relationship? Or perhaps even a plush toy your boyfriend won at a funfair for you at some carnival game? I know these are small things, but they are sentimental. The small things are often what make the difference between a good and a great relationship.

The element of sentimentality is what many modern couples miss or have never even experienced since the introduction of digital and online dating, smartphones, and social media. Romance back in the day was far more organic, and it wasn't shown through pixels or a heart emoji on a text message. In twenty years, the reams of text messages that couples shared will be irrelevant as they will be lost to time. Those messages on WhatsApp, Facebook, and other social media platforms will never be revisited. In all likelihood, those messages will probably be deleted by accident. However, a love letter or a polaroid picture is infinite and can be revisited thousands of times over. Don't get us wrong—we are all for the new age of dating and believe that the introduction of the internet and other forms of digital dating has made a world of difference. However, we would be lying if we say that we don't miss the way couples of the past made an effort with romantic rituals that have fallen by the wayside in modern times.

Modern Dating

As highlighted earlier, dating has evolved significantly over the last 15 or so years with the introduction of smartphones, the internet, and social media applications. Society has shifted from creating mixtapes of love songs for our significant other to swiping left or right on reams of dating profiles, hoping to get a compatible match. What is truly bewildering is that since the introduction of digital and online dating, some can argue that it is more socially acceptable (being the new norm) to slide into some stranger's DMs (direct messages) on Facebook or Instagram as opposed to asking out someone you met in line at Walmart for an innocent coffee date. I know it is absurd! However, this is how the world of dating has evolved (GDI, 2016).

To sum it up, although there are a lot of choices, with multiple ways to communicate with potential love interests on various platforms, there are still some critical restrictions in this online dating culture. However, in their entirety, social media, dating apps, and similar platforms have been crucial in breaking down various dating barriers that have hindered us as human beings from finding true love. Thus, even with its problems, it is still more beneficial than it is problematic. The philosophy of digital and online dating has broken down crucial dating barriers, such as geographical boundaries, time restraints, and lack of confidence in face-to-face situations. It has increased the number of potential matches we are exposed to. It now becomes easier to express one's sexual orientation and break down barriers of challenging career demands. It certainly does seem that love has become far more accessible and attainable for the average human since the introduction of smartphones, the internet, and social media applications. Here are six strategies to utilize digital and online dating to its optimum usage!

1. Know which dating app is right for you.

There are thousands of dating apps out there today, and you must know which app will fulfill your specific dating needs. Dating apps have oversaturated our app stores, and it seems there is a dating app out there for every niche in the modern day. It might sound basic, but knowing your niche is essential. Each one of these apps out there on the market has its own vibe, atmosphere, and purpose, and as such, they draw in a specific pool of people who use its app. Know the type of people you want to date, and from there, you will have a better idea of what dating app will work for you. There are tons of different themes for dating apps. Some are designed for DTF (down to f**k) hookups. Some are aimed at long-term relationships. Some are aimed at specific sexualities—like Grindr, for example, which is aimed at the LGBTQ+ community. Some are simply a mixture of everything. The best plan of action is to do some research on the dating app you are planning to sign up for before you become a member, as it will save you a lot of time and disappointment— not to mention dodging some very awkward situations (Joho, 2019).

2. Refrain from putting too much time and effort into digital chemistry.

The first thing we need to understand about dating on the internet is that whatever you type, text, or post does not directly translate to IRL (in real life) chemistry! This is something people get mixed up with all too often, and it is a grave error. We know how tempting it can be to get excited and raise your hopes up when you start chatting to a hot guy/girl you matched with on digital and online platforms. It's a great feeling, but don't get too carried away. The end goal is to ask them on a date where you can meet in person. Once you meet someone face-to-face, only then can you truly know if you guys get on like a house on fire.

The truth is that you could potentially waste days, weeks, or even months sending texts with a match online only to realize within a few minutes of meeting face-to-face that the spark is non-existent IRL. Various factors lead to people being attracted to each other, and you cannot comprehend them purely from text exchanges. You just can't.

Be careful if you have been talking to a hot guy/girl that you matched with on digital and online platforms for quite some time now. Do not build up unreasonably high expectations. This is because it will generally lead to disappointment. Oftentimes, the expectations you build in your head become almost impossible for your match to live up to when you finally meet IRL. So, don't be afraid to ask your match if they want to meet up IRL earlyish on (not too early) so that you can establish whether or not there is a true connection between you in person.

I tried online dating recently, and it is really refreshing. The ladies actually want to get to know me. Last night, one lady was asking me really great questions, like my first pet's name and the street I grew up on. She even wanted to know about my mom and her maiden name (Upjokes, 2021).

3. Ask for a quick video chat with your match before your non-digital date.

We understand that this can be daunting, and the very idea of a phone call can sometimes make us feel anxious. However, trust us—a three-minute video chat is a hell of a lot less painful than a two-and-a-half-hour awkward date where you play with the napkin the whole time and find yourself saying, "Nice weather we're having."

As mentioned earlier, there are a lot of factors that determine attraction between a couple that cannot be translated through texts, images, or voice notes. Memes won't help you here either, sorry. So what we suggest is for you to be brave and bold by asking for a quick little video chat to see if there is a connection between you and if you're ready for the real-life plunge (Joho, 2019).

4. Don't be so quick to judge a book by its cover.

This might sound a little strange since the whole purpose of digital and online dating is to simply judge someone off their profile picture and skim through their credentials to see whether they are someone you're interested in. We often fall into the trap of making quick judgments based on a person's profile, as we are often swiping left or right so quickly to save time. However, playing into our assumptions and swiping quickly can lead to missing out on potential matches that are worth our while. Another tip is to remember to read a person's bio and not just base your interests on their photos.

We need to acknowledge that people are not their dating profiles—they are far more complex than what 400 or so characters and a couple of pictures can portray. What we seem to ignore is that often bland or "boring" profiles are a product of people who are wet behind the ears when it comes to digital and online dating. We are talking about profiles that seem to come across as trying too hard, profiles that are a bit cheesy, forgettable profiles, and even profiles that come across as arrogant. These profiles can be pegged down to people who are not familiar with the dos and don'ts. It's just because some people aren't that great at branding themselves on a dating service. This does not mean they cannot be great dates in reality! The irony is often you should be more worried about people who have perfectly crafted dating personas, as this is indicative that they have been doing this for a long time and perfected the craft. Being active on a dating platform month on end is rather suspect, wouldn't you say (Joho, 2019)?

Our advice to you is just to be a little lenient when it comes to minor boo-boos, such as a couple of spelling errors, a corny joke, or a mirror selfie. We suggest trusting your gut as to whether or not you are interested. Hell, why not give them a shot to impress you in ways other than a mediocre dating persona? The worst that will happen is you guys won't click. In that case, you can simply unmatch and move on with your life, but at least you won't regret the "what if" feeling.

5. Do your research.

Yes, we already spoke about researching what dating app would work best for you as a person, but now here's your new research assignment. It is time to research your match quickly before you go on a real-life date. It can't hurt to know a little extra about your match other than what is on their dating profile before your date. However, make sure you know where to draw the line between curious and creepy. Just have a quick (I repeat, *a quick*) peek at their social media accounts. Firstly, you'll have more ammo in your arsenal when making conversation, and secondly, you'll see whether they are a person you are willing to commit your time toward.

Remember, it isn't creepy if your "research" is about staying safe and knowing what type of person you are about to have a coffee date with. However, it is creepy if you know every last detail about them and if you have visited your match's social media profiles 12 times in the last two hours. It is important to note that whatever you do find on your match online, take it with a grain of salt. People are wildly different from their digital and online persona, and we tend to forget that. According to a recent study, 76% of people spend approximately 15 minutes researching their match before their first date (Joho, 2019).

6. Be clear about your motive.

This is one of the most important and the most difficult rules to follow, yet we cannot stress enough how much time you can save yourself by simply establishing early on what it is you are looking for in a relationship. No, we are not suggesting that you have to confess that you are on the prowl and all you are looking for is FWB (friends with benefits) or you are looking for somebody's hand in marriage. Instead, what we are suggesting is that you frame the subject at hand in terms of mutual respect and open communication so that you and your potential match can have greater peace of mind, avoid disappointments, and lay down a foundation of honesty.

Modern Dating Glossary

Modern dating is quite complex. Thus, with the introduction of this new form of dating in the digital world, many new terms are commonly used that we need to become familiar with.

Breadcrumbing: Breadcrumbing is when somebody will send another person sporadic, however, noncommittal messages to another person. This is used to keep the spark of a dating prospect alive but on hold by utilizing minimal effort. It is almost like leading somebody on. It can be understood as somebody taking advantage of your hopes because as soon as you are ready to put an end to the connection, they just pop up again out of nowhere, keeping your hopes alive.

Benching: Benching is keeping another person on the sideline until further notice in case something happens to your current relationship or primary match.

Cookie-jarring: This is similar to benching, as cookie-jarring essentially means being somebody's side-piece. It is keeping somebody on the sideline as a potential partner in case something goes wrong in pursuing your primary romantic relationship or maintaining your current partner. With cookie-jarring, you are actively in contact with your side-piece, while with benching, you just keep them on the sideline as a potential plan B.

Ghosting: What ghosting essentially means is to completely disappear from somebody's life that you have been romantically interested in or somebody you are even in a relationship with.

Swiping left: Dismissing any chance of forging any type of romantic relationship with somebody in the blink of an eye. If you thought friend-zoning was the worst thing that could happen to you, think again.

Orbiting: Orbiting refers to somebody who isn't particularly part of your life or necessarily important to you but still goes out of their way to remain relevant in your daily lives. For example, if somebody is constantly liking and commenting on your social media posts, but they aren't ever really present in your physical world, then they are orbiting.

Paradox of Choice

Sometimes being spoiled for choice can do more harm than good. The same goes when we are spoiled for choice with so many options when searching for our life partner, boyfriend, girlfriend, or even a casual date. Unfortunately, having too many choices in this department can turn out to be detrimental (Abrams, 2019).

Today we are given so many options when searching for a partner online that we have almost created the illusion in our head that one match is disposable as there are so many other potential options. This is flawed thinking and can lead to some devastating blows and heartbreak if you are on the opposite end of the disposal. In this new era that has birthed a culture of dispensability, dating has become a game of window shopping, and relationships are being tossed away and recycled. This is not particularly healthy. The disposability of this era has often led to many people questioning their self-worth by second-guessing whether they are good enough or whether they could have done something "better." We need to understand that humans place greater value on things we have to work for and things that pose risks if we lose them.

However, although the illusion of disposability in the world of digital and online dating is cruel and takes some time to get used to, there are plenty of great opportunities to find love. The sheer number of couples and marriages that have been produced thanks to the opportunities of this method can be a testament to that (Abrams, 2019). Thus, we urge you not to be too despondent if a couple of matches go astray or if you find that you have been dismissed, as unfortunately, that will happen. However, if you set realistic expectations for yourself, adopt a healthy dose of self-love, and accept the fact that not every match or attempt to communicate is going to work out the exact way you planned it to, then you will be able to minimize the pitfalls of digital and online dating. Adopt these qualities and arm yourself with the knowledge about its reality and you will be able to date smarter. Do not compromise self-worth or emotional well-being for somebody you just met on the internet, as it just isn't worth it.

Chapter 2:

Flirt With Messages

Do you ever find yourself lost for words when it comes to texting your crush/match/boyfriend/girlfriend? Well, we have got you covered. We want to help you get the banter flowing in your next text conversations. Don't worry—we have all been there when we stare at the screens of our phones, wondering what to type for the perfect response or even wondering how to start a conversation other than sending a bland message like "Hey." We are sharing some of the top tricks, tips, and texting tactics you can adopt for your next text conversation to spark up the conversation while maintaining a flirty and lighthearted tone.

Tips for Getting the Banter Flowing (Leading Into Flirting)

When it comes to flirting, banter is crucial and is a great way to ease into a conversation that is both friendly and flirtatious. Dictionary.com describes *banter* as the exchange of playful and witty remarks in a good-humored teasing manner. The CEO of Select Date Society, Amber Artis, encourages couples and potential couples to begin conversations of a flirtatious nature with some clever and witty banter. Amber states that banter is always a good way to start a conversation. This is because the topics of banter are limitless, as you can pretty much converse about anything, whether it be about an actor, a sports team, a movie you have both seen, a musician, or even about a common experience you two have both experienced.

For example, if the two of you met on a dating app and you ask your match out on a date, you can flirtatiously say, "I'm keen for our date this Saturday night just as long as you solemnly swear that *Brooklyn Nine-Nine* is a way better series than *The Big Bang Theory*. Something along these lines will go a long way to keep your conversations with your crush or significant other friendly and lighthearted while still being flirtatious (Piñeiro, 2020).

Another important aspect that one should consider when engaging in witty banter is to keep the conversation short and simple. This is a tip from the CEO of Exclusive Matchmaking, Susan Trombetti. Susan says when you first start flirtatiously wooing someone you are romantically interested in, there is no need to send them long-winded paragraphs when texting. Susan suggests that you work your way up to deeper-level conversations as your connection with each other grows deeper and as you feel more comfortable with each other.

Remember, banter is about being funny and lighthearted, so don't forget to bring humor into the conversation. Many people enjoy using memes or GIFs to express themselves and break the ice when chatting with somebody they are interested in. In the 21st century, memes and GIFs have become a type of love language in the modern landscape of dating, so don't forget to use these tools in your arsenal when engaging in flirtatious banter.

Memes and GIFs aren't the only tricks up your sleeve that you can use. If you find yourself in a situation where you are struggling to come up with a response that is witty and flirty, you can always use some suggestive song lyrics to help express how you are feeling. Now here's where things begin to get spicy. If you find that the two of you have hit off through your online banter, you may want to find some erotic images of what you may be fantasizing to do with your boyfriend/girlfriend (or potential BF/GF) and then follow up the erotic image with a message "You down?" (Piñeiro, 2020).

However, when engaging in banter, there are a few things to avoid. When texting your potential love or match, remember to tone down on the emojis and use them wisely. Another tip to consider is to watch out when using too many exclamation marks. The best way to know if you are using too many emojis is to act out the message in your head. For example, if you are bold enough to send a kiss emoji, just send one, not six. Lastly, banter is about being witty, funny, and flirtatious, so make sure you are not being a Grinch or a Debbie Downer about things. Keep things positive, fun, and lighthearted—that is rule number one when it comes to banter.

Text Inspiration

Here are some flirty texts you can use once you and your match have established that flirty texting is appropriate:

1. "Hey, you! You are not going to believe this, but I had a dream about you last night, and all day I've been thinking about you. Can't wait to see you again!"

2. "Hey, I have got a fun question for you. What if we were trapped on a deserted island together—would you prefer to walk around au naturel, or would you insist we wore the same pair of clothes for months?"

3. "Hey, what do you think would be a cute emoji to put next to your name so it's saved on my phone?"

4. "I had such a great time with you last night! I can't wait to see you again soon."

Here are some text examples for matches or couples when both become more comfortable with each other:

1. "Your dress looks amazing, but it would look even better lying on my bedroom floor ;)" (This is best used as a response to an image someone sends you about their outfit.)

2. "I'm just lying in bed, and I can't stop thinking of how beautiful you are and how we were kissing so passionately last night."

3. "Hey, just thinking of the way you touched me on Friday night has got me feeling so excited ;)"
4. "Why don't you come over tomorrow night so we can Netflix and chill? Maybe we can even leave out Netflix."

8 Flirty Text Strategies

Flirting is a crucial part of dating. However, it is not as easy as everyone pans it out to be. Flirting is a lot easier said than done. There are a lot of negative thoughts that go through our heads when we plan on flirting with a romantic interest. Some of the anxiety that we feel can be accredited to whether we say the right thing or not. Will our attempts at being flirty come across as being cheesy? Will our attempts at flirting be misinterpreted? Will we come across as creepy? These are real problems that go through millions of people's minds when flirting, as the truth is flirting does not come as naturally to some as it does to others. Flirting is hard enough, but flirting and over text is even harder at times. This is because your match/crush/BF/GF cannot even see your facial expressions nor hear your tone of voice over a text. However, although some may view digital and online flirting as more difficult than real-life flirting, there are a lot of positives when it comes to flirting over text. For instance, when digitally flirting, you have more time to think of a response and have the opportunity to craft the perfect thing to say. On top of that, the physical barrier can reduce the jitters and anxiety you may feel IRL, thus allowing you the opportunity to open up more than you would in person.

When sending a flirty text to someone, you can let them know that they are on your mind even when you are apart from each other and going about your daily life. Flirty texts will help you open up the conversation in greater depth and lighten the mood, as well as help you set up the all-important next date. However, what is daunting about text flirting is sometimes you don't know what to say. It isn't a secret that you want to come off as confident when you flirt with somebody over text, but you also don't want to come across as too overbearing. You want to be funny but not too cheesy. The best way to ensure your confidence and humor through means of flirting is to not overthink your texts too much and remember to keep them short and sweet. Here are eight flirting strategies with great examples you can use for your next flirty convo (Entenman, 2018).

Strategy #1: Be bold and ask a flirty question.

1. "Hey, I've got a saucy secret. Wanna hear it?"
2. "There's something I don't understand, and maybe you can answer it for me: why are you so damn cute?"
3. Hey, I don't know about you, but I'm in the mood to have some fun. What about you?"
4. "I was wondering, do you prefer when somebody makes the first move or not really?"

5. "You know, every time I see the kissing emoji, I think of you. I was wondering which emoji makes you think of me."
6. "Our first kiss is going to be magical. It's going to be like something straight out of a movie, don't you think?"

Strategy #2: Boldly express how much you like the other person.

1. "You never fail to make my heart sing with joy."
2. "I've enjoyed getting to know you. You are getting more awesome by the minute."
3. "Getting a message notification from you always makes me smile no matter how bad my day is going."
4. "Every minute we text, the world is just confirming that I have found my dream guy/girl."
5. "You're the first person I think of when I wake up and the last person I think of when I go to sleep."

Strategy #3: Remember to reference the last time you both were together in person.

1. "I can't get over how beautiful you looked last night. I've been thinking about it all day."

2. "Last night was the most fun I have had in ages. I can't remember the last time I laughed so much. Thanks for such a great date."

3. "I've been in the office for four hours already and haven't gotten a single thing done yet because I can't stop thinking of that kiss last night."

4. "I've never had so much fun bowling before. I guess it must be a great company."

5. "I'm so glad I got to share watching *Avengers: Endgame* [replace with any movie you currently saw together] with you."

Strategy #4: Reference the next time you will be together in person.

1. "I loved our date last night. I had the best time! I cannot wait to do it again soon."

2. "Hey, my week is looking quite relaxed. Do you want to make plans? How is yours looking?"

3. "You are going to love the outfit I picked out for tonight for our date this weekend. I can't wait to show you!"

4. "It's so cold. I wish you were here to cuddle with me. Maybe this weekend we could cuddle and watch movies."

Strategy #5: Be brave and make plans.

1. "Hey you, I get off work early on Friday. Do you want to go get some drinks once I leave the office?"
2. "Ever since you mentioned sushi, I haven't stopped thinking about it. Do you want to go grab some with me tomorrow night?"
3. "The brand-new Pixar movie is out. You know I'm a sucker for animation. Do you want to see it with me on Saturday?"
4. "There's this new coffee shop that opened a few blocks away from me. Do you want to try it out with me?"

Strategy #6: Be selective and witty with your emojis. Remember, there are more emojis in your arsenal than the eggplant and peach.

1. "Do you feel like {pizza emoji} or {burgers} for our date next weekend?"
2. "Are you more of a {cat emoji} or {dog emoji}?"
3. "You are as beautiful as a {rose emoji}."
4. "{Heart eyes emoji}—this is me every time I see your face."
5. "Hey, I just want to say you're as sweet as {honey pot emoji}."

Strategy #7: When you're more comfortable with each other, don't be afraid to get a little PG-13 or even R-rated.

1. "Hey, why don't we exchange selfies and rate who's cuter?"
2. "I hate being in my bed alone without somebody to cuddle with. I can't wait to cuddle again with you."
3. "I had a frisky dream about you the other night, and I can't seem to get it out of my head."
4. "What are you wearing? It's so damn hot. I'm au naturel at the moment . . . just saying."
5. "I can't stop thinking about all the amazing things we could be doing if you were here at my place right now."
6. "Everything you do, no matter how small it is, never fails to make me want you more."

Strategy #8: Say what is on your mind.

1. "I was just listening to the new Ed Sheeran song, and it reminds me so much of you."
2. "Hey, my dogs seem to like you more than me. I can't blame them."
3. "I only have 5% battery life left on my phone, but there is no other person in the world I'd rather use it to talk to."
4. "I just wanted to tell you that you look beautiful. I know I can't see you right now, but

you're always beautiful, so right now is no different."

5. "Hey, are you thinking about me as much as I have been thinking about you lately?"

Various Other Flirty Text Tips and Ideas

Why is it that when we are chatting to our best friends over WhatsApp, Facebook Messenger, or any other texting platform, it feels like the easiest thing in the world? When we talk to our best friends, the most natural, charismatic, and humorous side of our personality radiates. However, when we talk to our crush or a match we secured on Tinder or Bumble, we find it difficult to barely string a sentence together, let alone a flirty sentence. Strange, isn't it? This is the dilemma that millions of people across the globe struggle with. It's ironic that we can be effortlessly funny and charismatic with our friends, yet at the exact moment when we actively try to be our charismatic and funny selves, our true personality eludes us.

How often have you wanted to be as casual and funny with your crush, just like when you are with your friends, but your mind overanalyzes a situation and you crack under pressure? It's no secret because we have all fallen victim at some point in our lives. We have all stared at our phone screens for minutes, sometimes hours, trying to think of the perfect response, but it never comes, so instead, we reply with a very dry "ha-ha" message. We know that texting your crush can spike your anxiety. It can be difficult to break the ice with your potential partner, so we have provided some sassy and witty conversation starters that will help you pique your crush's interest (Laurence & Robinson, 2020).

1. Show that you're paying attention.

Showing your crush that you are acknowledging them and that they pique your curiosity is vitally important when letting your crush know that you are interested. After all, how are you ever going to get your crush's attention if they don't think you are interested in what happens in their daily lives or they don't know that you are thinking about them outside of your texts?

Example: "Hey, Mike, you were incredible in your basketball game tonight! Woah, you really know how to get a crowd riled up with those epic three-pointers of yours. Maybe one day you can teach me to shoot like you."

Result: There are two major benefits to a message like this. Firstly, your crush will be super chuffed that you attended their basketball game, and secondly, they would be extra happy that you noticed their great shooting form on the night. You also opened the opportunity for some bonding time in the future by asking your crush if he will help teach you how to shoot one of these days.

2. Get a debate going.

Getting into a friendly/goofy debate with your crush or boyfriend/girlfriend is a great way to give your conversation legs. It gives the conversation so much room to expand, and within the debate, there is so much to talk about. Debates don't need to be serious; they can be on wacky off-wall topics. The more lighthearted the debate topic is, the better. When a debate topic is lighthearted, there is ample opportunity to bring humor and banter into the mix, and your convo can go on for hours.

Example: "What goes first, the milk or the cereal? Choose wisely, as we might have found our first deal-breaker ;)"

Result: This is a very lighthearted and casual debate about something incredibly silly (it's literally about the anatomy of cereal). However, it is a funny topic that can be discussed in length for quite some time. It is also bound to include some humor and some banter. So try to make your crush laugh. Humor is our best wingman/wingwoman.

3. Check in.

Remember to check in with your crush and ask how they are feeling (even if it is something small) just to show them that they are on your mind. This helps show your crush that you truly do care about them. Just make sure you draw the line between checking in with your crush and pestering your crush with multiple clingy messages.

Example: "Hey, I didn't see you at the office/college today. Are you feeling alright? If you need anything, just shout {hug emoji}."

Result: This will mean a lot to your crush as it shows them that you noticed they weren't around and that you missed them. It also shows them that you were concerned that they might be sick. On top of that, not only were you concerned, but you took the time of day to check in with them to see if everything was okay and offer assistance if needed.

4. Show off your skills.

Dating is about self-branding, and there is no better way to brand yourself than showing off what you are good at. Show your crush that you are unique and that you have talents. These unique skills and talents are bound to pique their curiosity and get their attention focused on you. Show them why they should choose you as opposed to somebody else.

Example: "Hey, do you like pasta? I just found this new pasta recipe that I am dying to cook. Do you wanna be the judge?"

Result: Showing off to your crush that you can cook will entice them to come over. Also, you will also be offering them a free meal, and who doesn't love eating for free! On top of that, you know what they say: the quickest way to somebody's heart is through their stomach. If you can't cook, that's fine, but don't be afraid to show off what you're good at.

5. Amp up anticipation.

Make your crush excited to see you. Build up the suspense and make it seem like it is worth their while to spend time with you. Keep hinting at how great it will be next time they will see you and that you have something exciting in store for them.

Example: "I just saw the best horror movie! I know you love horror. I can't wait to show it to you tomorrow. You are going to love it."

Result: Your crush will be so excited to see you next time in person because they would be super interested in seeing this great horror movie you just saw and would love to experience it with you, especially because they are a fan of the genre. It gives your crush something to look forward to.

6. Send your crush memes.

Memes are so vitally important in today's culture, especially when it comes to banter. As mentioned earlier, banter is crucial when it comes to digital and online flirting, and in today's climate, memes have become a love language. Memes make everything better and are a great way to lighten the mood. If you find a meme funny, send it to your crush. One better option is to send a meme that you know they would enjoy (an inside joke or a fandom they enjoy). Even if it is a meme related to something you guys said to each other recently, send it. Memes are highly relatable and a great way to get a conversation going and lead to flirtatious banter.

Example: "This meme is so you!" (Insert a meme that is relevant to your crush's personality.)

Result: You will get them laughing and pique their interest with a meme. Humor, like food, is a way to our hearts.

7. Invite them to events.

Get your crush involved in your life as much as possible, and it is even better if you can get your crush on good terms with your friends. If you guys ever get into something more serious, your significant other and your friends must get on. It will save both of you very awkward encounters if your friends are on board with your relationship and your potential partner doesn't loathe your crew.

Example: "Hey, me and the guys have an indoor soccer match this weekend. I would love it if you would cheer our team on. Afterward, we can get pizza :)"

Result: Your crush would be honored that you thought about them and wanted them to join you for your soccer match. Plus, they would be stoked to catch some pizza with you and your friends after the game for a chilled post-game dinner.

8. Ask for recommendations.

Asking your crush for recommendations shows them that you value their opinion and you want them to be involved in your life. It also shows that you are acknowledging that they have great taste when it comes to common interests and they are the go-to person when asking for advice on food, movies, music, series, etc.

Example: "Hey, I just finished watching *Schitt's Creek*, and I need a new series. I know you love your sitcoms. Any recommendations?"

Result: This shows your crush that you value their knowledge of sitcoms and that you trust their judgment when asking for recommendations. Plus, it gives you something to talk to them about once you have watched the show they recommended since they have already seen it.

9. Use food.

As said earlier, food is a quick way to the human heart. It is always a winner. Food is often our secret weapon. I mean, who doesn't love food after all? Get to know what your crush's or potential lover's favorite food is and use it in your favor. Perhaps make it an enticing reward in a friendly competition over text.

Example: "Let's play 21 questions to see who knows each other better. The loser has to take the winner out to their favorite pizza joint!"

Result: This is a playful competition that is not only lighthearted but also fun. There is also a prize to be won at the end. If you can cook, then entice your crush with the awesome dishes you can prepare as this will not only show your bae that you got skills but also shows that you want to spoil them.

10. Use fun nicknames.

Nicknames are awesome, and they are a great way to show your crush that they are uniquely important to you and not just another number on your hitlist. It makes your connection personal and adds depth to the affection you guys feel for each other. Who doesn't love a good nickname? Just make sure the nickname you give your crush is affectionate and not belittling.

Example 1 (personal touch): "Hey, you're so cute and cuddly. You remind me of Yogi Bear. I think I'm going to call you Yogi from now on."

Example 2 (more generic): "Hey, cutie, how are you doing on this lovely Thursday evening?"

Result: Whether you decide to call your crush cutie (more generic nickname) or Yogi (more personal nickname) is purely up to you. However, a cute nickname adds that flirty and sweet touch to a message that makes the receiver of your text feel warm and cozy inside.

11. Use your adorable pets.

Who doesn't love a cute cat or dog, right? Well, we sure do, and we are part of the vast majority of the world, so let your pets be your wingman/wingwoman. Use your pets as an excuse to get your crush/boyfriend/girlfriend to come over and hang out, or at the very least get a conversation going over text. Send cute pictures of your pets over text and have a contest with your match/BF/GF to see whose dog is the cutest.

Example: "Bubbles keeps asking for tummy rubs, but she just isn't satisfied with mine. She doesn't enjoy anybody's attention more than yours. I keep telling her you will be back soon to give her your world-famous tummy rubs."

Result: Your crush will be flattered to hear that your dog/cat is missing them, and they would be more than happy to come and spend the day with you and your dog. Perhaps you could take Bubbles (your pet) for a walk with your crush, which could even lead to a romantic picnic in the park.

12. Bond over common interests.

Having common interests with somebody is a vital component to establishing any type of relationship, romantic or otherwise. Although the saying goes opposites attract, it is also important that you have some things in common. Not only is having common interests with your potential or current romantic interest important to sustaining a balanced relationship, but it is also a great way to start a text conversation. Texting about common interests can lead to a conversation that goes on for hours, giving you and your partner/crush plenty to talk about. This can be anything from movies, TV series, books, music, sport, and many more interesting passions.

Example: "I can't believe what I just watched! Did you watch the season finale of *Stranger Things*? It was crazy. You have to watch it."

Result: You guys will have a lot to talk about *Stranger Things*. You could possibly tell each other how you both thought the season would end or even give your take on an alternative ending. You could talk about your favorite characters or similar shows like the one you both are watching. You could even give crazy fan theories about the show. Honestly, talking about common interests opens a whole wave of opportunities.

Chapter 3:

Picture-Perfect

We said in chapter 1 not to be so quick to judge a book by its cover, but that doesn't mean your profile picture is not important. When it comes to constructing the perfect profile, picking a great profile picture to brand yourself to potential matches is vital to the success of securing quality matches. We understand that choosing the perfect photo is a lot of pressure, particularly if you are the kind of person who is picky with photos of yourself. However, don't fret too much as major platforms regularly construct in-depth surveys to find out exactly what other users are looking for and what pics catch their eyes. Thanks to the results from these surveys, participants from around the globe will be in a far better position when having to choose their perfect profile pic to garner the attention of millions of singles worldwide (Bates, 2017).

Tips for Flirting on Social Media With Photos

In the modern tech-savvy world of dating, we need to find just the right balance between the dreaded art of flirtatious subtlety and shamelessness. Get this intricate balance wrong, and your whole attempt of wooing the next "love of your life" will blow up in {flame emoji}. We need to understand that in our attempts to woo an individual, we cannot go too big, or else we will be labeled that "thirsty" creep before we have even entered their sacred DMs. However, if we don't go big enough and play it too safe, then the heart eyes emoji that you sent to your crush will be long forgotten under your crush's many other more aggressive digital suitors.

To become the modern-day Romeo, we must think like the modern-day Romeo. We need to learn all the secrets out there to help improve our game on social media without falling victim to either extreme (going too big or too small). First things first: know how to flirt with your images.

1. Keep your photos fresh.

If you have chosen social media as your primary hunting and dating ground, then treat these profiles with the same love and attention as you would if you were using a dating app. If this is the avenue you have chosen, the first rule is to have a killer profile pic. Make sure your profile pic is a recent picture of you and that it is flattering. Also, make sure your profile pic is your main identifier and is key to drawing attention from others. Thus, it needs to be highly focused and not some grainy pic that looks like it was taken on a phone in 2006.

2. Avoid "deep-liking."

Digital and online dating isn't so different from flirting in real life in the sense that you want to make your intentions clear to your crush, but you also don't want to come across as desperate, creepy, or overly obsessed. Thus, the rule applies to social media also. There's no harm in peeping down the rabbit hole of your crush's social media account; just make sure you are only looking and not double-tapping a pic from 267 weeks ago. Once you start double-tapping or commenting on posts from months or years ago, you are crossing the border to creep territory and you don't want to be there. Deep-liking or commenting on ancient posts is the modern equivalent of stalking (DMARGE, 2020). Think of it like parking outside someone's house, waiting for them to walk out the front door just so you can see them. Yeah, it's kind of like that, just digitally.

3. Notice signs of reciprocation.

Take a minute to notice if there is any reciprocal communication between you and your crush. For example, if your crush begins to like and comment on your post, it is a positive sign that they may be into you. At the very least, it shows you that your crush is interested enough in you to take action on your posts, possibly because you initially took action on their posts. If you find that your crush is interacting with your posts, then you have been given the green light to take the next steps in seducing them over social media. Perhaps it is time to slide into their DMs. However, this tip is very important, so listen up. If you continue to pursue your crush online and you see they have shown little to no signs of reciprocating, then hang tight. Either give them space to reply or give up on your flirtatious venture. Do not be that person who sends multiple DMs/texts to somebody who is not replying to you. More importantly, do not become aggressive if they haven't replied. Just move on.

4. Don't send dick pics!

For the love of humanity, please leave your Johnson off of all social media conversations because, trust us, it is NEVER a good idea. There is no bigger crime to flirting than unsolicited dick pics. Even if they are solicited, we suggest you don't partake in the exchange of any genitalia images. However, some dating apps and social media are specifically designed for hookups, so in those cases, we guess it is okay. Just be very cautious when practicing the dark art of the dick pic. On top of not sending dick pics, do not leave inappropriate or "thirsty" comments on somebody's posts, as this is just cat-calling behind a screen. Just for your protection, stay clear of genitalia or nude images. These may leak out to the general internet!

5. Apply the Great Gatsby effect.

Believe it or not, you aren't the only person trying to slide into your crush's DMs. That's just the truth, and there is no way around that. You are competing with tens of people to get the attention of your next "one and only." Thus, you need to stand out, and sometimes you need to make that special somebody you are trying to impress jealous.

That's where the Great Gatsby effect comes in. With this flirting technique, you are aiming t0 show that special someone how great a time you are having without them (DMARGE, 2020). You are enabling their jealousy; thus, you are playing on their desire to want you even more than all the other digital flirty companions they have mustered up. To put the Great Gatsby effect to good use, post a video, photo, or story that all of your followers can see but in a way that is curated particularly for your crush to lay eyes on. This way, when your crush sees your post/story, they will see the good time you are having and all the fun they are missing out on when they are not with you. For example, if you went to a party that was super fun, play it up and make it seem like it was the party of the year. If you recently went on an awesome vacation, make your crush think, "What if I was there with him?"

What to Avoid When Picking the Perfect Dating Profile Picture

There are many aspects to consider when picking your profile pic to portray yourself. However, there are also many aspects to avoid, and here they are:

1. Photos with your ex: Having any photos with your ex on your profile is an absolute no-no! Pictures with your ex send a negative message to any potential match that you are still not over your ex and you still have a sentimental and emotional attachment to them. It sends a message to your potential matches that your attention still lies with your ex and that you view your matches as side pieces, rebounds, or bandages for your wounds of unresolved history. It doesn't matter how attractive or awesome you seem in your profile picture. If it looks like you are not over your ex or, worse, you are still in a happy monogamous relationship, you will scare away potential matches. People don't want to be seen as second best or have to deal with your emotional baggage.

2. Photos of your face are nowhere to be seen: Your profile pic is your identity. If nobody can see your face, it is rather suspicious and a little creepy as it makes it seem like you have something to hide. People want to know who they are talking to, and by this, they mean they want to be able to put a face to the name behind the screen. You should include at least one or two photos of your face out of the five or six pictures you are allowed to upload. Having a beautiful sunset or ocean backdrop is awesome. However, make sure they do not take up your entire profile (Bates, 2017). People want to see your face. How else will they be lovestruck by your dazzling smile or kind eyes?

3. Obvious and over-the-top image manipulation: People like authenticity. Daters want to see the real you. They are not interested in your Photoshop skills, and they certainly won't be impressed with abs that have been obviously placed on your shirtless body through image manipulation.

4. No obnoxious gym selfies: Avoid taking gym selfies. We know you worked hard for your body and spent hours in the gym, but posting a gym selfie, unfortunately, runs the risk of coming across as a little self-obsessed. You are also most likely to look sweaty and tired in a gym selfie since you have just finished a workout, and that isn't a good look for most people. On Tinder, it is found that gym selfies result in 5% fewer matches (Bates, 2017).

5. No old photos: Avoid using old photos, and what we mean is don't use photos from over a decade ago. Photos from two or three years ago are fine—just don't get older than that. Nobody wants to see your photos on a 4-megapixel camera from your phone in 2008. Plus, people age, and nobody looks the same as they did ten years ago.

6. No sunglasses: Sunglasses are awesome—don't get us wrong. However, they shouldn't be used on your dating profile. Our eyes are the window to our souls, and when you wear sunglasses, you have drawn the curtains that block the window. Our eyes help create genuine connections, and besides that, sunglasses can send a subconscious message that you're trying to hide something.

Being Attractive Is Not a Requirement for Digital and Online Dating

Let's talk about the elephant in the room. Do you need to be attractive to get matches on internet dating platforms? No, and we are dead serious when we say that attractiveness is not a deal-breaker in the world of digital and online dating! The irony is that on some platforms, being highly attractive can be your downfall when dating on the internet. It was found on the dating platform OkCupid that highly attractive people ended up receiving few matches (Bates, 2017). This was especially true for men using the app. The study further found that men who would generally be considered as average or below average in looks were more likely to receive messages from potential matches from women. However, attractiveness is a very subjective matter. Labels such as an "average-looking" person for one person could be someone else's "very attractive-looking" person and vice versa. To be blunt, the attractiveness that your profile picture portrays is unlikely to be the main reason that your dating profile is looking dry. According to eHarmony, an attractive profile pic may start a conversation, but it is your personality that will carry the conversation and form genuine connections (Bates, 2017).

When and How to Use Selfies on Dating Profiles

The selfie has become such a common occurrence in our daily lives in modern times, and it is a photo technique that has become second nature in the 21st century. However, is there a place for it in the world of digital and online dating? Well, unfortunately, not really. That is if you're a male. On the other hand, females that use selfies on their dating profiles garner more positive results. According to the London School of Medicine, the most effective pictures for women to use on their dating profiles to secure matches are selfies with their heads slightly tilted to one side (Bates, 2017).

However, the study also found that men who use selfies to brand themselves on dating apps are 8% less likely to secure matches than male profiles that don't upload selfies. If you are going to use selfies, here's a tip. When utilizing the technique of taking selfies, make sure your face can be seen in the photo. According to Tinder, a selfie that incorporates a full shot of your face will up your matches by 27% (Bates, 2017).

What we would suggest is to utilize full-body shots on your dating profile as they are always a winner, and 86% of both men and women would agree with us. Medium shots that include your face and torso behind an alluring (but not distracting) backdrop are also very effective and should be something to consider when constructing your dating profile. Full-body and medium-body photos are effective, as they give your matches a clearer idea of what kind of body type you have.

Just keep in mind that you should not take these full-body or medium-body shots in front of a mirror. It's a no-go. According to the dating app Zoosk, women are a staggering 29% less likely to swipe right on your profile if a mirror selfie has been uploaded (Bates, 2017). Make sure you don't make the even bigger mistake of uploading a bathroom selfie as the damage is critical. The same study by Zooskflavor found that bathroom selfies are 90% less likely to be swiped right on!

How to Use Profile Pics to Lead Into Conversations

They say a photo speaks a thousand words, but how do we turn those words into conversations? Those who cleverly pick their profile pics can start a conversation through their photos. Let's discuss what photos can help you do just that!

If you are a man, then we suggest you use a photo of yourself outdoors. According to studies, it is found that men who upload pictures of themselves in the outdoors are 19% more likely to receive right swipes or likes as it shows potential matches that they are putting in the extra effort (Bates, 2017). A study conducted by eHarmony also found that photos that portray your interests are also far more likely to start a conversation as it gives your match something to talk to you about. Perhaps you may even share common interests/hobbies, such as hiking, sports, traveling, or cooking.

Dogs are another great way to get your conversation started. Everybody loves a cute dog. If you have a cute dog, share it with the world. Let them admire their cuteness with an adorable picture of the two of you. Let your dog get the conversation rolling.

However, be wary of posing with your cat as a study found that you are 53% less likely to be swiped right on with a picture of your cat than you are with a picture without your cat (Bates, 2017). For women, be cautious when posing with your dogs on your dating profile, as it was found that women were less likely to be swiped right on when posing with their dogs. The same study found that the interests that men find most attractive in women and that will secure more right swipes include art, growth, family, dancing, and health/exercise. Photos that include these attractive qualities on a woman's dating profile will not only secure more right swipes but also get the conversation started with their matches.

Lastly, men and women love food, so don't be shy to upload a photo of yourself at a restaurant, smiling over a plate of delicious sushi.

Are Group Photos Appropriate for Dating Profiles?

Group photos are not a deal-breaker on dating profiles. However, they are not advised to use in abundance. One is fine. We know many people include group shots on their dating profiles as many of the photos you take are with your friends. However, the problem is group photos can cause confusion, and you may end up being lost in the crowd. Imagine if you matched with somebody, but they thought they matched with one of your friends in your group shot. Pretty awkward, right?

However, as we said, having one or two group photos is acceptable, as they can help demonstrate that you are a likable person and you have an active social life. They even prove that you aren't just another dating profile bot that oversaturates the digital and online dating world (Bates, 2017).

If you do have a group shot with your friends, make sure it isn't the primary pic (first pic that shows up) on your profile. This is because group photos confuse people on the other side of the screen who are viewing your profile for the first time. They might not know which person in the shot is you! Don't overcrowd the shot. Keep the number of people in the photo to a minimum, and don't have more than four people in one photo. Digital and online dating is a game of speed and quick swipes. If you have a group photo on your profile, make sure you stand out. For instance, if you have red hair, post a picture without any other redheads in the photo.

Take note, if a group shot is the first photo on your profile and they can't identify who it is they are swiping right on, chances are they won't take the time to look at the rest of your profile.

There is an exception to group photos that can work to your advantage in digital and online dating, and that is a group photo with your family. This is because it shows you are close with your family members, and both men and women find close family units an attractive quality. Just make sure your family photo isn't some cheesy Christmas card. A study found that uploading a photo posing with your mother improves your percentage of securing a match by 7% (Bates, 2017).

Should You Smile for the Camera?

Say "Cheese!" Well, some will say you should smile for the camera, while others will argue against that and prefer a more natural photo. For women on a digital and online dating platform, a flirtatious smile aimed specifically at the camera is often given the green light. It is believed that when a woman smiles in their profile pics, potential matches subconsciously garner a connection when locking eyes with their potential female match.

The goliath dating app Tinder found that smiling in your photos increases your match rate by a staggering 14%. So next time you upload your photo, consider showing your pearly whites (Bates, 2017). Just make sure your smile is authentic and not some forced, unnatural grin. Moreover, make sure you do not pout (this is not 2013), as pouting is universally considered a turn-off in the modern world of dating.

According to a study, women are 47% more likely to smile in their photos than men are. Statistics further found that it is to a man's advantage that they smile less than women do in photos. The same study found that men are considered to be more attractive when they are looking away from the camera, thus giving the photo a more natural ambiance. However, make sure you still have a few photos of you smiling on your profile, guys! The study further found that showing your eyes, regardless of gender, is crucial in strengthening connections with potential matches (Bates, 2017).

What we suggest is to do what you feel is natural—there is no right or wrong answer. However, we would advise you to upload at least one or two photos of you smiling on your dating profiles.

Get Somebody Else to Take Your Photo

Unfortunately, there's only so much we can do when taking a selfie, and generally, it just ends up being a close-up shot that looks like a mess. If it isn't a super close-up shot, then it is a selfie in front of a mirror, which is also a no-no. So, we suggest you be brave and ask your friends if they can take a photo of you so that you can get a better photo of yourself with great depth and range. You could also even hire some professional help and spend a few bucks on a professional photographer to stand out more. However, we are aware this may not always be feasible. You could also buy yourself a selfie stick to ensure your selfies have a little more flavor (PicMonkey, 2016). What we are trying to say is, don't be afraid to ask for help when sourcing your perfect profile pics.

Tasteful Edits

There is nothing wrong with a little editing. Just make sure they are subtle and not obviously manipulated, where it becomes overkill. Here are some tips to make sure your photos look just right.

1. Cropping: Cropping is a useful technique when editing your photos as it can put greater emphasis on you at the forefront of the photo, enhance the composition of the image, and change the image's orientation (landscape shots were found to be a winner according to eHarmony). However, do not use cropping techniques to crop out your ex in one of your photos. Not only is this a bad idea as somebody may find the original photo, but cropping out another person in a narrow portrait shot generally does not perform well on dating apps.

2. Touch-ups and filters: Touch-ups are fine as long as they aren't taken overboard. Be careful not to overuse the dreaded airbrush tool to touch up your face. Making small touch-ups, such as brightening your eyes or removing stray hairs, is all good to highlight our attractiveness. The problem happens when we start to remove every little blemish or fine line from our faces. When we airbrush our faces to an untasteful degree, we start looking like characters from a PlayStation game more than we do human beings. If you want to edit your photos to get a more natural look, make use of the touch-up tab in the editing option with features such as adjusting the brush size and adding a little fade here and there. The trick is to do minimal touch-ups rather than overhaul the image entirely. If you are still not feeling your photo, try fixing it with a filter. The filters we suggest you use are Urbane, Focal Soften, Intrepid, or Fancy Focus (PicMonkey, 2016). So, next time you feel the urge to touch up your photos, remember that sometimes subtlety is key.

3. Photo quality: Make sure your photos are of high quality in terms of resolution, as this is very important. eHarmony found that photos that have poor quality or that are too small can seriously halt your chance of success in the highly competitive world of digital and online dating. Take a hard look at your photos before you upload them, and if they aren't looking like they fit the bill, then we suggest that you look at whether the dating app that you are using provides the ideal dimensions for your photos on their platform. For instance, match.com suggests that all photos uploaded on their platform should be 300✕400 in dimension, so if you are using Tinder as your primary dating app, then find out what dimensions they suggest (PicMonkey, 2016).

Chapter 4:

Video: Secret Tricks That

Nobody Is Using

With the COVID-19 plaguing the world and long-distance relationships becoming a feasible option due to technology, it is no surprise that video dating is playing a major factor in our society at the moment. There has been a recent surge in online dating due to these factors. On the dating app OkCupid, matches have spiked since the start of the COVID-19 pandemic, leading to many online conversations taking place. A lot is happening over video calls too. Thus, the COVID-19 pandemic has seen a massive surge in digital dating in general. We are living in an era where we are advised to stay put in our homes, making video dating an even more appealing and viable option to our dating needs in the current climate we are living in. In response to "the new normal" that we have been forced to follow, dating apps have been rolling out awesome video features to help keep our romantic needs alive without putting people under unnecessary (and possibly fatal) risks of participating in an in-person date (Sharabi, 2020).

Benefits of Video Dating

Video dating may not be the same as an in-person date. We know it can be a little overwhelming at times, but that doesn't mean it doesn't have a lot to bring to the table. One of the major benefits of video dating is that it creates a sense of social presence. Creating a social presence is incredibly important when trying to make somebody feel comfortable and close around you (or on-screen with you), not to mention how important it is to create a meaningful connection with somebody. When you have a video date with somebody, it can feel far more real. It can almost feel like an actual date, except you are just separated by a screen. It feels more like there is a real person beside you compared to, say, text messaging someone.

Another benefit of video dating is that it can keep us safe during a global pandemic by eliminating the risk of going on in-person dates with our loved ones. We know this isn't ideal, but we are living in an unprecedented era riddled with one of the deadliest pandemics the world has ever faced. On top of that, video dating is also highly beneficial for the thousands of people in long-distance relationships who want to feel close to their partners but can't because of geographical limitations. Luckily, with the help of video calling, long-distance couples can feel close together once again no matter where they are in the world.

Another major benefit of video dating is that it helps extend the process of getting to know somebody on a deeper level compared to text messages and voice notes. When two people participate in a video date, they have granted themselves the opportunity to spend more time talking and getting to know each other (without distractions) before deciding to rush into a physical/sexual relationship. Video dating may even save you lots of time and disappointment. Think of it as an audition. Through video chats, you can get to know somebody far better than you can via text; thus, through a video date, you can phase out any person you feel you will not click with on a date in real life. This can save you from a very awkward first date. Remember, video dates can give you a far better idea about a person's experiential qualities that make them attractive, such as their confidence and sense of humor, thus limiting surprises later on in the relationship (Sharabi, 2020).

Call us crazy, but we think that even after COVID-19, video dating will be here to stay and will be the next evolutionary step in the world of online dating.

Tips for Using Video for Your First Date

As mentioned earlier, we are living in an era of self-isolation due to the effects of the dreaded COVID-19 pandemic. Thus, we are advised not to go on in-person dates as the risks are simply just too high. Thus, during this COVID-19 pandemic, we either try to self-isolate or maintain at least six feet of distance from other people. Thus, given the current climate we live in, there isn't much alternative other than a video chat when going out on a first date. If you have been dating somebody for a while already, it is different, but for a first date, it is probably best to keep it digital. However, even without the pandemic, there are other reasons why you would want to keep your first date digital. The first reason is sometimes people's pictures are a little too good to be true. Before you meet a stranger in person, you might need some further clarification to identify whether they are who they say they are. Secondly, you may have just met somebody online, and they could potentially be far away. Before you drive all that way, why not see if you guys click first through a video date? Lastly, you may have a crazy work schedule, and you want to connect with somebody before your match loses interest in you. Whatever it is, video dates are handy tools for first dates, and here are some vital tips to increase your success for your digital first date.

1. Learn how to set up a video date via a dating app.

So you think you have just matched with Mr./Ms. Right. You feel you two have hit it off, and you want to ask if they would be keen on a video date. The truth is, asking somebody on a video chat is far less risky or nerve-racking than asking somebody out on an in-person date. This is because it is a much smaller ask than asking them to meet up in person. Remember, the smaller the ask, the higher chance of success (Zirby, 2020). Remember, on a video date, there is far less risk involved for things to go wrong or to get extremely awkward. After all, they can just hang up if they aren't feeling the date. However, on an in-person date, it is far more difficult to just bounce. Thus, a person who is not too keen to meet in person may agree to a video date since the risk of things going wrong is low (Zirby, 2020).

We suggest you follow these three tips when asking your crush/match on a video date:

- Ask sooner than later. Don't let their interest in you dry up.
- Be casual about it. Remember, a video call isn't that big a deal.
- Keep the call short to take the pressure off them. Let them know you only have a few minutes to chat.

It's important to note that if somebody is willing to chat on video, then it is likely they are warming up to you and want to meet in person in the future.

If you notice your match is not shy to get to know you, asks a lot of questions, makes use of emotive language and exclamation marks, and is simply engaged in the conversation, then it is a good time to ask them on a video date. The best plan of action to do this is to simply be straightforward and ask a question. Be bold and ask if they want to continue the conversation through a video call.

Here is a great example of what you could say: "Hey, I've really enjoyed our conversation. What would you say if we picked this up through a video chat? We don't need to worry about social distancing. I'm free now. How about you?"

2. Do NOT call out of the blue!

This is important, so listen up. We know you may be excited to hop onto a video call straight away once you have acquired your match's contact details. However, even if you feel like everything is going well, beware of just calling out of the blue. It can be very invasive, aggressive, off-putting, and creepy, especially if it is late at night! Remember, you need to respect other people's time and understand that they will not always be available for a chat. On top of that, if you guys are not in a committed relationship yet, then the dynamic is incredibly different than if you were going steady for a year already.

3. Set a 10-minute time limit.

Remember, just as you are feeling nervous about your video on the first date, so is the other person on the other end of the line. If you don't set a time limit, the other person may be worried that they will be stuck in an awkward long video chat, and that can be off-putting. It is important to note that anxiety around going on a video date for the first time can often be amplified as you can see the other person, and the potential for all kinds of weird things can happen with the camera turned on (Zirby, 2020). However, there is a way to reduce their anxiety, and that is to limit your first video date to only 10 minutes. This will make the other person feel far more comfortable. It also takes away some of the anxiety from you and your date. So the next time you set up a video date, tell your match that you are only free for 10 minutes. You will find that people will be far more willing to jump on a video chat with you. On top of that, after 10 minutes, you will leave the conversation at a high point instead of an awkward goodbye where you have run out of things to say. You will also leave your date wanting more, creating ample opportunity to set up a follow-up date.

4. Use the call-back method.

The question many people ask is, how do we make a natural transition from a dating app conversation to a video chat date? The answer turns out to be quite simple. The best technique to use in this situation is known as the "call back" method (Zirby, 2020). To utilize this method, all you need to do is reference something from your dating app text conversation as soon as they answer the video call (of course, say hello first). If you don't know what to reference from your text conversations, then reference something from their dating profile. For example, if their profile says they love to travel, then bring something up that is related to traveling. Perhaps ask where their dream destination is. By doing this, you not only break the ice and feel more familiar, but you are also showing your match that you took the time to look through their profile. Voilà, an easy transition from text/video chatting.

5. Use open-ended questions.

Remember, this is a date, not an interview. **Don't opt for interview-style questions.** When you fall into the trap of rapidly asking question after question to your match, it makes the conversation feel one-sided.

Avoid these types of questions as they are overused and bland:

- "What hobbies do you have?"
- "Hey, what have you been doing today?"
- "What do you do to keep yourself busy during the day?"
- "How was your day?"

We understand that logically these questions make sense. However, logic doesn't always have a place in online dating—emotions do. These questions are all right if you are more comfortable with each other or perhaps you meet in person, but remember you have only set 10 mins for your first video chat, so you want those 10 minutes to get sparks flying.

We suggest if you are going to ask questions, make sure that they are open-ended. Look to ask questions that simply cannot be answered with one word. That way, both of you will have a chance to talk, and the conversation will not be hogged by either one of you.

For example, these open-ended questions will keep the conversation interesting and elicit more than one-word responses:

- "What would you say was the riskiest thing you did in the past six months?"
- "I see you love traveling. What is the next destination on your hitlist and why?"
- "What is the funniest experience you and your friends have together?"

There are three reasons you would use open-ended questions on your first video date. First, they keep your date invested. Second, they keep the conversation rolling and keep it interesting. Third, they allow both of you to have the chance to talk. Open-ended questions are great as they act as a rabbit hole for your conversation (Zirby, 2020).

6. Use the golden phone call for video.

The "golden phone call" is an awesome technique that you can use on your first video date as it 100 percent applies to that situation. The point of this technique is to get the other person attracted to you by having an incredible time with them over a video chat. There are two very important elements to the golden phone call. The first is to be playfully skeptical, and the second is to utilize the humble brag (Zirby, 2020).

Attractive women have an ocean of men that are constantly on their tail trying to meet up with them, and because of this, many women have to worry about factors, such as:

- What if this guy is just another creep?
- It's one thing if he is creepy, but he could be dangerous too.
- What if this guy reeks of desperation and things get awkward fast?

Thus, this will run through the head of many, many women in the world of online dating. As mentioned before, setting a 10-minute time limit on the call is one way to remove that anxiety. However, there is another option, and that is to be playfully skeptical. An example of being playfully skeptical is as follows:

"Hey, I was wondering if you wanted to video chat, but I must be honest, you seem to be too good to be true, which is a bit suspect. You sure you're not some 65-year-old man who lives alone with 12 cats?"

Asking something along these lines is lighthearted and shows that you are flipping the script by being playfully skeptical. This also shows that you understand the fact that women get bombarded by creepy dudes all the time. It also shows that you're socially smooth. You don't reek of desperation, and the fact that you have the confidence to screen out girls indicates that you have other options.

Now the second element of the "golden phone call" is the humble brag. Now, this doesn't mean you have to be an obnoxious fool who thinks way too highly of themselves and views others as lower-class citizens. It simply means sharing with your match what your life is about (Zirby, 2020). The point of the humble brag is to highlight the most positive aspects about yourself while still maintaining an element of humility. The trick here is that your humble brag should be balanced, and what this means is that your brag should include a little self-effacing. Use the humble brag in your 10-minute first video date to impress your date without coming across as obnoxious.

Important Tips for Your Video Date

1. Use proper lighting.

Setting the right mood and getting your aesthetic just right is the ultimate mood setter for any date. That's right—even for a video date. The first thing we are going to want to do is to integrate daylight in our video date. Daylight is our friend in this situation. We suggest you do your video date near a window during the day, as this will give your date some natural light, which will not only make the picture clearer for your date but will also make your skin look a lot better (Zirby, 2020). If you video-call at night, then just make sure you are in a well-lit room. We also suggest you have a quick camera check before your date to make sure you don't look like you're in a 1960s movie.

2. Keep your background neat and tidy.

Yes, we know you might not care if your room is in a mess, but your date just might. So it's better to be safe than sorry. Remember, if your background looks like a mess, then you might come across as an untidy/unhygienic person, and you don't want that. We suggest that for your video date you choose a neutral setting, such as in the living room that is looking spick and span or perhaps outside on the patio with some flowers and trees in the background.

3. Wear proper clothes.

We shouldn't have to tell you the next tip you should consider, but we are going to tell you anyway: please wear pants. We know it is a video date, but some etiquette and effort are still required. What happens if you need to stand up for some reason? Anyway, just wear your pants. It's not asking much, and it may just save you from utter embarrassment. If we are being honest, we suggest you go a little bit further than just wearing pants. Just because you aren't meeting your date in person doesn't mean you shouldn't treat it as a date. No, you don't have to wear a suit and tie, but it is important to still give your date the impression that you care about how you look and you know how to take care of yourself (Zirby, 2020). It wouldn't hurt to brush your teeth right before the call so that you are certain that there is nothing stuck between your pearly whites and that you can wow your date with your dazzling smile.

When picking what outfit to wear for your video date, remember that your clothes are an extension of your identity and can speak volumes about you. Whatever you choose to wear, make sure that the clothes are wrinkle-free, are in decent shape (no stains or rips), and fit your body type well. It is also important to note that you should dress for the camera. For example, solid colors are a good choice as they are often less distracting than clothes that have busy patterns (especially stripes) and color schemes. We suggest that you stay away from clothing that has slogans, busy/large logos, or clothes that incorporate fluorescent colors. Lastly, you are going to want to make sure that your clothes don't blend in too much with your backdrop. The last thing you want is to look like a camouflaged chameleon with just your head floating around. Remember, you want your date's attention to be on you and not your clothes, but you still want to come across as presentable. Avoid slouching, as this can make it seem like you are trying to hide something or that you are just uninterested in the conversation.

4. Get your angles right for your video date.

If you decide to use your computer as the device you are going to have your video date on, then making use of an external webcam is your best bet, as it will provide you with more control over your positioning and angles used during your video chat. We suggest that you make the camera eye level with you, as this will give you the best results. However, if you are making use of the camera built into your device, then try your best to position your computer so that you are aligned at eye level with the camera (Vida Select, 2020). When you are talking, look at the camera as this will create the illusion that you are maintaining direct eye contact with your date. What you want to avoid is having your camera positioned too high or too low in relation to your face, as this will distort your features and make your face and upper body look unflattering. Not to mention you will lose the illusion of maintaining eye contact, as you will either be looking up or down.

If you decide to use your phone as the device for your video date, we suggest that you experiment for a couple of minutes before the date to find out the most flattering angle for your features. Once you have found what angle best suits you, hold it in that position during your video date. This way, your phone camera is at optimal positioning before the video date has even commenced. Lastly, just before your video date, do a quick check to see if your camera is working properly and that everything looks good on-screen (Vida Select, 2020).

5. Eliminate potential distractions.

Remember, your first video date can be as important as your first in-person date as it is the first time you will be seeing each other "live." You want to be able to control the environment as much as you can, as even missing the smallest of details can prevent you from achieving a successful connection. To eliminate risks of potential mishaps, it's best to eliminate as many potential distractions as you possibly can. You don't want to give your date the idea that they are competing for your attention. The best way to do this is to choose a quiet location for your video date. Choose a location where there are no rowdy children, barking dogs, blaring music, and noisy roommates. Also, make sure the TV is off. If you live with roommates or children, try to find a time when they are not around so you can have your video date without any distractions. We also suggest wearing headphones during your video date, as it will help you hear your date more clearly and block out any outside noise that could potentially distract you.

6. Think outside the box.

Get creative and be unique. Look, there is nothing wrong with having a little Netflix and chill with your partner every now and then, but there is so much more that you guys can do over a video date. See chapter 5 for more ideas. Why not learn something new together by taking a MasterClass? Perhaps you can go on a virtual tour of all the best museums across the globe. Or maybe you're in the mood to break a sweat and have a gym session together. Honestly, the possibilities are endless.

7. Learn something about each other.

Why not use your video date as an opportunity to get to know each other a little better? No, we are not talking about interrogating each other and firing rapid interview questions but instead getting to know each other through lighthearted games. Play 21 questions with each other. Maybe you can tell each other embarrassing experiences or share little-known facts about yourselves. Another great game is "two truths and a lie." The rules are simple: each one of you tells two truths about yourselves and a lie, and you have to guess which one of the three answers you gave is a lie. Not only is this a great ice-breaker, but you will learn a little bit more about your partner each time you play while still having fun (Strong, 2020).

A Little Verbal Affirmation Is Always a Winner

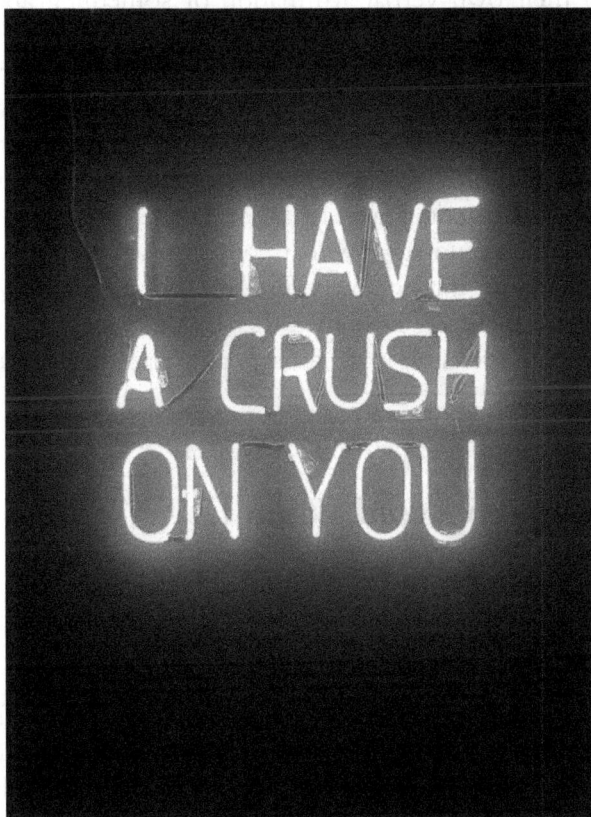

Do not underestimate the power of verbal affirmation and flattery. However, just remember that if you want your compliments to have a positive impact, it has to be genuine. Thus, don't say anything that is obviously insincere just for the sake of flattery, as your date will see right through that (Strong, 2020). Take notice of the small things that your date does that are worth praising, and you may just find that your date will reciprocate with their own verbal affirmation of something about you. Compliments are great—they will not only make your date feel good but also spark a flame and inspire a flirtatious atmosphere to your date. Compliments will make your video date feel a lot more like a date in real life. Don't go overboard with the compliments, though, as you may come across as desperate or insincere. However, we do suggest that you throw in a couple of compliments throughout your date. For example, you may comment on how nice their home looks or how their hair looks so nice today. You may even praise their humor.

Things to Avoid When Using Video for Your Date

Just as there are things we need to include in our first video date, there are also those that we need to steer clear of. Here are things that you should always avoid:

1. Resist the urge of being negative. Do not complain. It isn't attractive, and it is rather off-putting.

2. Don't put yourself down or be overly self-deprecating, even if it is just for a joke. It makes it seem that you don't believe in yourself, and you may come across as weak.

3. Don't be so logical. Loosen up. Logical conversations can get boring and make people lose interest, especially if they don't understand what you are saying.

4. Avoid falling into the trap of rapidly asking questions. This can make somebody feel uncomfortable and can signify that you are nervous.

5. Do not fidget. It makes it seem like you are very nervous, and it can make your date feel uncomfortable.

6. Do not chew gum during your date. Nobody wants to see that.

7. Do not stare at yourself in the camera. We know you look good, but staring at yourself comes across as being vain. Maintain eye contact with your date instead.

Chapter 5:

Virtual Dating Ideas

The internet has opened the world of opportunities, and it has also provided the human race with the necessary tools to maintain and build upon remote long-distance relationships from across the globe. With the introduction of the internet, relationships can be formed from all facets of the globe. Somebody living in Wales can be in a happy and healthy relationship with somebody living in New Zealand. This is all thanks to technology and the impact it has played in breaking down geographical boundaries in the dating world. We also need to remember that the times we are living in are crazy, and we are living amid a global pandemic, suffering the effects of the dreaded COVID-19 virus. Since March of 2020 to date, we have been encouraged to practice social distancing and isolate ourselves from people around us, including our romantic and potentially romantic interests. Thus, virtual dating ideas are needed more than ever both for long-distance relationships and even relationships where both partners live in the same city.

Long-distance love is thriving due to the current situation humanity finds itself in. Thus, it would be wise to get creative about keeping the spark ignited with your partner or potential partner. Today, people are quarantining with their boyfriends/girlfriends/dating app matches through digital means. With technology such as Zoom, WhatsApp, and other dating apps, you can stay in touch with your loved ones even if they aren't physically with you. Hell, you can even have an entire virtual date over a video call with your partner in your underwear. We know it is a strange time we live in, but it is not without its opportunities. We live in an era where we pretty much undergo most of our daily activities, so why not bring dating into the virtual space to keep your long-distance and pandemic romance alive?

Below are some awesome ideas that you and your match can do to keep the fire burning in your relationship from a distance.

Look for Virtual Museum and Exhibit Tours

Ever wanted to tour some of the most renowned museums and exhibits in the world in your pajamas? Well, now you can! You can go on a virtual tour of the Louvre, Madame Tussauds, the NASA exhibit, the National Women's History Museum, and many more exciting exhibits from the comfort of your own home with your partner. Museums and galleries are always a classy date to take your loved ones. You and your partner can digitally gaze upon the *Mona Lisa* in awe. You can go on a guided digital walk through the Smithsonian Museum of Natural History. You can be dazzled by beautiful Renaissance artwork at the Getty Museum (Groner, 2021). The opportunities are plentiful, and it makes for one jam-packed culture-filled date you and your partner can experience together, thanks to technology.

Stream Your Favorite Artists' Concerts

Who doesn't love a good concert? I'm sure between the two of you, there are at least two or three artists you both enjoy and sing their songs in the shower. With the internet, you can both enjoy your favorite artists' concerts together through a virtual space. Hundreds of artists from various genres are constantly performing worldwide. Some are superstars on the biggest stages, and some are less well known. It doesn't matter because, in the 21st century, you can stream their concerts live. You and your partner can bring Coachella to your living room and stream all your favorite artists while you jam to them together. Grab your flower crown and neon lights, and make a fort and enjoy the stay-at-home festival you and your partner have curated for yourselves (Groner, 2021). We suggest that you keep an eye out for the next concert of one of your favorite artists. When it's available, stream it together so that the two of you can have an awesome music-filled date that will be one to be remembered.

Want to be a little more personal or intimate? Make each other a Spotify playlist and share it with each other. Once you both have listened to each other's personally curated playlists, you can discuss them and get a conversation going.

Try Dinner Delivery Roulette

This one is one of our favorites. We have already mentioned that food is the quickest way to the human heart, and we wholeheartedly stand by that. For this virtual date, you will exchange each other's addresses and will be tasked with the responsibility of ordering takeout from your favorite restaurant for your respective partners. You will let your partner know what time they can expect the delivery to arrive, but you cannot tell them what food they will be expecting. The aim of this virtual date is to order one of your favorite dishes from your favorite restaurants to be delivered to your partner's door. Once the food has arrived at both your addresses, you will both unbox the takeout together and enjoy each other's favorite foods. Not only is this super cute, but you will also have a lovely dinner date with your partner over a video call.

Watch a Live Stand-up on You-Tube

Who doesn't love a good laugh? Laughing and humor are so important in any relationship, and there is nothing better than laughing uncontrollably with your partner or potential partner. Luckily for all you love birds out there, the extremely talented Marissa Goldman hosts weekly live stand-up performances from new up-and-coming talents from across the globe. This comedic experience is fully digital and takes place weekly on YouTube. These highly talented comedians want to bring laughter to all involved in a pandemic-friendly format, and what's more is there is a no drink minimum (Groner, 2021). Join in on the fun with your date by digitally attending the performance for a whole new lockdown-friendly heckling experience. It is not only a great idea for a date during a pandemic but also a fantastic dating option for your long-distance partner.

Host a Trivia/Game Night

Board games are going digital! Today, virtual board games of all our household favorites are popping up everywhere. Games like Cluedo, Monopoly, Risk, Catan, Scrabble, Game of Life, and Trivial Pursuit all have digital variants. Why not host a game night with your partner or potential partner and battle it out virtually with a game of Risk? Trivia is another fun date option. You could even host a pub quiz against each other. It will be as if the two of you were grabbing a drink at the pub.

Use Netflix Party and Chill

If you haven't downloaded Netflix Party yet, then do yourself a favor and download it. It is available on both Android and Apple's app stores. This app is the perfect way for you and your partner to enjoy a movie together, even if you are separated by geographical boundaries. Netflix Party enables you and your partner to sync your devices so that your video-viewing experience is synced with each other. You will see what they are seeing, and they will see what you are seeing. Netflix Party also enables a live chat option between whoever is watching together, and you can also share your live reactions based on the show you are watching together. We know it's not the same as being able to cuddle together on a cold night while you binge-watch *Friends* for the fourth time, but it is still a great way to enjoy a movie or series with your loved ones from afar.

Get Sweaty With a Virtual Gym Sesh

It's time to get sweaty with your partner. Get the body moving by live-streaming yoga and meditation training routines. There are thousands of different routines that are constantly being uploaded by fitness trainers from all over the world, making it super easy for you and your partner to work up a sweat at home. Schedule a gym session with your partner and have a fun and active date. Not only will both of you get fitter, but you will be able to motivate each other to push yourselves to new physical levels.

If you feel like spicing things up, there are plenty of dance-based workouts online that you and your partner can try out together. Make working out feel like a party by grabbing your brightest and most over-the-top neon gym wear. Clear the dance floor (well, your living room), connect to Zoom, and get the endorphins going with a dance-filled exercise (Groner, 2021). Shake what your mama gave you.

Level Up! Sharpening Your Skills Together

It's time to level up, and what better way to improve upon yourself than doing it with your partner. Take a MasterClass with your partner and learn something new together with the help of a guru in whatever field you feel like you both can benefit from. Perhaps you want to sharpen your cooking skills? Then there is no better teacher than Gordon Ramsay himself, right? Join a cooking MasterClass with Gordon, and next time you guys see each other, you can wow each other with your new and improved cooking skills. If you are feeling romantic, why not take a MasterClass with the legendary poet Billy Collins so that you can write each other poetry and woo each other with your beautiful words? What's more, MasterClass has a "buy one, get one free" special that often runs, so it is as if it was built for couples in mind (Groner, 2021). The world is your oyster, so learn something new together with a MasterClass date that is filled with knowledge.

Perform a TikTok Dance

TikTok has proven itself to be one of the biggest phenomena of the 21st century. It has literally changed the world. Some love the platform, and some don't, but one thing is for sure: TikTok has proven time and time again that it can bring people together no matter where they are in the world. You can't mention TikTok without mentioning TikTok dances. Love them or hate them, they are here to stay. So why don't you and your partner learn a catchy, cute little TikTok dance that you both can master and post for the world to see? It is fun, lighthearted, and goofy and is a great way for you and your partner to pass the time on a fun-filled date. There are literally thousands of different TikTok dances, with new ones being choreographed as we speak, so pick a dance and perfect it with your partner online.

Take a Fakecation

We know traveling is a no-no at the moment, and even if it wasn't, traveling is expensive. However, that doesn't mean you and your long-distance boo can't scratch your travel itches. Thanks to the introduction of technology, you can travel the world digitally on a stunning "fakecation" with your partner, similar to the virtual tours of museums and exhibits that we mentioned earlier. Many tourist attractions have jumped on board with virtual tours as they are aware that traveling is a no-go during a pandemic. So you and your boo should virtually hop and digitally roam the streets, beaches, sites, and natural wonders the world has to offer. Digitally visit the Colosseum in Rome, tour the Pyramids in Cairo, and enjoy the Berlin wall right from your coach. Fakecations come with an added benefit because sometimes relationships aren't at the stage of going on a real vacation together; thus, a fakecation is a great way to test the waters (Drillinger, 2020).

Create a Dating Pinterest Board

Get even more social! Make a board on Pinterest that both you and your partner have access to. Use the Pinterest board as a board to plan future dates with some fun and cute ideas that the two of you can share in the future. The board can be filled with both physical and digital dating ideas. Think of it as a visual to-do list. This will help both you and your partner feel optimistic about what is still to come out of your relationship together. Pinning up cute dating ideas gives both of you something to look forward to, and it also means that you are both contributing to the well-being of the relationship, which is crucial. Not only will this Pinterest board help amp up excitement, but it also means you will have loads of awesome ideas when you meet up in real life again (Drillinger, 2020).

Exchange Recipes and Do a Cook-Off

We're sorry to keep bringing up food, but we cannot stress it enough when we say how important food is in not only attracting people but also enhancing a strong connection with somebody. So, here we go again, except this time we are talking about recipes rather than the food itself. For this virtual date, you would need to create a document on Google Docs that is shared between the two of you. In the document, you would continuously add new recipes that you both already use or recently acquired. Then as a date night, the two of you will video-call each other and pick one of the recipes on Google Docs. You will then both cook the chosen recipe together in your respective kitchens. Once the preparation is done, you will have a lovely dinner date over a video call. You can discuss the recipe and decide whether you liked it or not. Maybe you can talk about whether you would have done something different with the recipe. You can even make it a competition on appearance (since you can't taste each other's finished product through a screen). You can make it so that whoever cooks the dish that looks the most appetizing gets to choose the next recipe for the next cook-off.

Start a Two-Person Book Club

This date is for all you readers out there. You and your partner pick a book that you both enjoy and then schedule a timeframe that works for both of you so that you are reading at the same time and finish the book at the same time. Then choose a day of the week when you two can discuss the book in-depth, such as what you liked and didn't like, what you would change, or even conspiracy theories. Just make sure you both are on the same page in the book or that you have both finished the book before discussing it to avoid any nasty spoilers. The virtual book club for two is kind of like binge-watching a series together, but it requires a little more effort and lends itself to deeper and more in-depth conversions (Sager et al., 2021).

Share Photo Albums

Nothing quite captures a moment like a photograph, and every great relationship has moments that couples want to keep to showcase their love for each other. So, why not create a collaborative photo album on Dropbox so that both of you can add and scroll through your awesome photos together whenever you want? Alternatively, one of you can create a photo album on your phone filled with all your fun-filled moments so that the two of you can scroll through them once you love birds see each other again in person. A shared Pinterest board is another alternative. You both can even walk down memory lane by including old photos from your childhood (who doesn't love a cute baby picture or photos from your school years?) (Sager et al., 2021).

Send Care Package

This is a really cute and creative idea for a long-distance relationship that we strongly urge you to try out. Send your partner a beautiful custom care package to let them know that you're always thinking of them no matter where they are in the world. Send them a bottle of wine or a six-pack of beer and have a night out on the town for some drinks. In the care package, leave a note that reads "Drink? 19:30?" Then hop on to a video call and have a fun night of drinking with your partner even if they are miles away (Sager et al., 2021).

Drinks are just one of many ideas. The options of what you include in your care package are endless. You could even send your partner a vacation through delivery. Yes, we know this sounds odd, but just hear us out. For instance, if your partner has always wanted to visit Paris, send them a beret, baguettes, croissants, some fine wine, and then call them on Zoom with a backdrop of the Eiffel Tower and have a lovely virtual dinner in Paris. If you want to be b0ld, you can surprise your partner with a real trip to Paris during your virtual dinner (provided COVID-19 has eased up, of course).

Keep One, Discard the Other

This is a lighthearted yet hilariously fun game that you and your partner can play with each other over a video date. Have you heard of the game "Would you rather?" Well, this is a pretty similar game. In this game, you and your partner will hilariously expose each other's core identity values in a fun and non-judgmental manner. In this game, both of you will be given two options, and you will have to pick one option that you will keep forever and another option that you will decide to discard for life. We suggest you start off easy, such as the simple option of pancakes or waffles. You will have to choose whether to keep pancakes forever and discard waffles from the face of the earth or the other way around. Progressively make the option more wacky. So next could be pillows or blankets. Next thing you know, you will be arguing whether to keep sex or the penal system in this upside-down future you and your partner are designing (Groner, 2021). Just remember not to judge, and all answers are valid and in the spirit of the game. Try to steer clear from offensive or political choices and just make the options as wacky as you can.

Get to Know Your Cosmic Compatibility

Get to know your crush/boyfriend/girlfriend on a cosmic level by learning what their star, sun, and moon signs are. Who knows, you might learn a few things about each other based on what the stars have foretold. Start off by searching your signs online to see your common character traits in relation to your respective cosmic signs. Then have a friendly discussion on whether you agree or disagree with what the cosmos has to say about you (Sager et al., 2021). Once you both have a good idea about what your cosmic signs are and the type of traits that are generally common to people of these signs, then it could be fun to see if the cosmos considers the two of you romantically compatible. Again, you can read up on what the stars have to say about your cosmic compatibility and then discuss what you do and don't agree with it.

Just remember, if you are going to do this, don't hold what you read on the internet close to your heart. After all, it is just a blog/article written by a person who doesn't know either of you from a bar of soap. Although cosmic signs do provide certain insights into a person, it is far from accurate and should not be the defining factor regarding whether you and your partner are compatible. Have some fun and see what the stars have to say about you two, but take everything with a pinch of salt.

If you two are feeling even more inquisitive, you could test the waters even further and participate in a virtual couple's tarot card reading. It is believed that tarot cards can provide some further insights in relation to love and can assist you and your partner to further improve upon your connection with each other. However, just like your cosmic compatibility, tarot readings are by no means foolproof, so if you choose this option, don't get too worked up about what you learned about each other if the reading wasn't quite what you expected.

Chapter 6:

Best Mobile Apps for

Finding Your Match

There are so many dating apps to choose from that it can sometimes feel overwhelming when trying to decide which one would suit you best. That's why we wanted to narrow down your options by highlighting the best dating apps that we feel are the most relevant in today's dating climate. We have included various dating apps, all with unique twists and features that distinguish them from their competitors. We have also highlighted a range of different dating apps that have marketed and positioned themselves to align with the preferences and needs of various markets. There are apps that cater to millennials, LQBTQ+ men, LQBTQ+ women, people looking to settle down and get married, apps that cater to single parents, and many more apps with unique and interesting features that draw various types of people. There may be more than one app that catches your fancy. Try them out. Take them for a test drive to see how they perform for you!

How to Build the Perfect

Dating Profile

As you can see, the world of digital and online dating is complex, and there are tons of factors one needs to consider when venturing forth into the world of modern dating. However, what is truly important is knowing how to construct your dating profile, as this is your brand and what differentiates you from the millions of other users you are competing with to grab the attention of the next love of your life. That's why we have compiled some super handy tips to help curate your perfect dating profile:

1. Ask a friend for some assistance: Nobody quite knows you as well as your friends do. Heck, sometimes your friends know you better than you know yourself. If there is anyone who can help portray the perfect you, then it is your friends. Writing your bio can sometimes be the toughest part of digital and online dating. We often don't know what to say, or we are too worried to come off as obnoxious, stuck-up, or corny. So why not ask your friends to help you write your bio? We are sure they will know how to market their friend.

2. Avoid clichés: Be original and think out of the box. Nobody wants to hear how you love to take long walks on the beach. We have all heard it a million times. Even if you do enjoy drinking a glass of red wine with a book in front of a dancing fire, leave it out of your bio (Proudfoot, 2020). It's used too often, and quite frankly, the world wants to hear something unique, fun, and interesting about you. When writing your bio, try to make it something you haven't heard before, and try to make it witty. Puns are always winners.

3. Look at other profiles for inspiration: Sometimes we have a bit of a mental block. We get it; we've all been there. However, there is a trick to break down the wall of your mental block, and that is to find inspiration from other people's dating profiles. Take a look at what other people are saying about themselves and see which bios catch your eye. Once you have sampled a few profiles for inspiration, use them to help spark an awesome bio for your own profile (Proudfoot, 2020).

4. *Capture action shots:* Include an action shot as one of your profile photos, as they are known to up your chances of being swiped right on. What we mean when we talk about an action shot is something along the lines of a photo of you skateboarding, doing gymnastics, skiing, or even rocking out on your guitar.

5. *Check grammar:* Poor grammar and spelling is a turn-off for many people, so best be on guard when writing up that perfect bio. We know even the best of us make mistakes, so don't be too hard on yourself. However, just be careful and have a second read-through before you upload your bio. If you aren't naturally good with spelling and grammar, don't fret too much as you always have your buddy Autocorrect by your side (Proudfoot, 2020).

6. *Have fun:* It's no secret that most people want to find somebody that is funny, fun, and outgoing. So, we suggest you brand yourself as being that carefree person with a great sense of humor. Making someone laugh through your profile is not only a great way to be noticed but also a fantastic conversation starter.

7. *Be honest:* Lying will not get you very far in the dating world, as people will quickly see through your lies. Plus, just remember that there is another human being on the other side of the screen whose emotions are not some plaything to be toyed with. Just imagine how you would feel if somebody you were dating straight up lied to you and played you for a fool. So, just be honest and true to who you are.

The Best Dating Apps Available

Tinder (IOS and Android)

Tinder is arguably the most popular swiping dating app available. Tinder is a dating app that encourages its users to make quick judgment calls on other people's profiles during their search in finding their new potential partner. Once you join Tinder, you will create a dating profile, which is quite basic. Upload a few photos on your profile to help stand out, and accompany your photos with an interesting bio (a couple of points/sentences) to increase your match rate success. Once that's done, you will launch yourself in the spotlight with thousands of other singles in your area and battle it out to garner each other's attention through swiping. With Tinder, you will either swipe left on a profile that does not interest you or swipe right on a profile that you feel aligns with your preferences. There is another feature called "super liking" in which you swipe up to increase your chances of matching with somebody else even more. However, you will only be able to message another person if you both swipe right on each other, and even if you super liked them, they will still have to swipe right on you before you can begin talking.

What's great about Tinder is that they are always looking to innovate and stay with the times. Recently, the goliath dating app rolled out a video feature that now allows its users to make in-app video calls. This removes the need for both parties to exchange sensitive contact/personal details, which is incredibly important for safety issues, and it also aligns with the social distancing era of COVID-19. What is even more significant is that Tinder has provided a crucial Safety Center feature that provides its user with a panic button. It is used to notify others if you feel you are in danger on a date. There are also talks that Tinder is looking to introduce a feature that allows for background checks of potential matches, allowing you to pull data from public sources to ensure your Tinder experience is safer. This feature limits your risk of potential danger (Corpuz, 2019).

Tinder is primarily for male and female single millennials. The main purpose of Tinder is to assist singles in forming potential new romantic relationships with other singles in their area. However, Tinder is also often used to get to know awesome new people in your area and form great friendships.

Tinder offers a free version for their users but also has an optional premium version, known as Tinder Gold, which users can subscribe to for added benefits. Tinder Gold is best for users between 18 and 30 years old, as there is a discount up for grabs for any user that falls into this age bracket. Tinder Gold is $6.92 a month for a year for anybody between the ages of 18 and 30. The subscription price per month is more expensive for users over the age of 30. Tinder Gold offers a range of benefits, such as unlimited swiping, one free boost a month, five extra Super Likes a day, no intrusive advertisements, and permission to connect immediately with anybody who swiped right on your profile. Some tips to stand out on Tinder include having a witty bio, refraining from being too serious, not being afraid to message your match first, and uploading pictures that are natural or at least show you have a bit of a goofy side to you.

Bumble (IOS and Android)

Like Tinder, Bumble is another goliath in the world of dating apps. Bumble is similar to Tinder, as it also makes use of a swiping system. However, there is a catch. With Bumble, both users will swipe left or right on each other as usual, but once two profiles swipe right on each other and they have matched, only the female in the equation (the queen bee) is able to send the first message. Thus, Bumble has flipped the script. Instead of the guy making the first move, as we have been so socially conditioned to believe, it is now the ladies who have been tasked with that responsibility. However, you are on the clock, and once you match, you only have 24 hours to send the first message before the connection between both profiles is lost forever. The 24-hour time applies to both the female's first message and the male's first response. Once both parties have sent their first message, the connection will stick, and there will no longer be a time limit for further messages throughout your connection with each other. However, if the connection is of the same sex or you have signed up for the BFF feature, then it is up to either person to make the first move within the next 24 hours, or else the match will disappear. With the premium option of Bumble, you can get another 24-hour extension.

Back to the BFF feature. What Bumble has done is they have offered a feature designed to help you find friends, not to find romantic relationships. Just like Tinder, Bumble continues to be innovative by offering video-calling features and a brand-new Night In feature. The Night In feature is really unique and allows matches to participate in games, such as trivia night, giving you and your potential partner something engaging to do while on a video date together (Corpuz, 2019).

Bumble is primarily for male and female single millennials. The main purpose of Bumble is to help singles form potential new romantic relationships. Bumble is also often used to find friends by getting to know awesome new people in your area. Bumble offers a free version for its users, but it also has an optional premium version, known as Bumble Boost, which gives users added benefits. Bumble Boost is $8.99 per week or $24.99 per month. Bumble Boost boasts loads of added benefits, such as five SuperSwipes per week, unlimited swiping, rematching with a match that expired after 24 hours, gaining a 24-hour extension with your match, the ability to revert accidental left swipes, and Spotlight (make yourself stand out more). Here are some tips to stand out on Bumble: Don't be afraid to talk about yourself in your bio. Keep your photos recent. Do not overly edit your photos. Make sure your first photo is the one that stands out the most. Diversify your pics with your hobbies and interests to showcase who you are—don't have five selfies of you smiling in the same location.

Hinge (IOS and Android)

Hinge is an incredibly popular dating app among millennials, and it is designed with the focus to help aid you with finding relationships and engaging in interesting conversations. The unique element of Hinge is that it is designed to be an app to be used for a short period. The app is marketed in such a way that it encourages the user to delete it sooner rather than later—presumably because you have found love online thanks to its features and you are no longer in need of its services anymore.

Unlike Bumble or Tinder, Hinge does not make use of swipes and instead opts for more detailed profiles that are made up of uploading more images and sharing interesting stories to get your conversation moving. Users can like or comment on the images, regardless of whether you matched with another user, and this acts as a great way to get your conversation rolling with another user. Every day, users are given recommendations about other users whom the app feels best aligns with what they are looking for. Hinge has also introduced a feature known as Standout, which will highlight other profiles they feel are your type and provide you with topics they feel will help bring a conversation to life with your potential match.

Hinge has responded to the COVID-19 pandemic by teaming up with Chipotle and Uber Eats so that you and another profile can enjoy a virtual dinner date together through their video call feature. Hinge has also been found to have high statistics for going on second dates (Stodart, 2020).

Hinge is primarily targeted toward both male and female single millennials. It is used to help singles meet other singles in their area to assist them in forming potential relationships. While Hinge has a free version, it also has a premium version, known as Hinge Boost, that has many added benefits that their users can subscribe to. Hinge Boost is currently set at $19.99 per month. Hinge Boost has awesome benefits that include no intrusive advertisements, unlimited swipes, the ability to view everybody who "liked" you, and advanced preferences to help you on your search for the one. Some top tips to stand out on Hinge include uploading photos that inspire conversation and elicit comments, making use of a witty bio, making the first move, and being brave by liking or commenting on other profiles' pictures.

eHarmony (IOS and Android)

eHarmony is a seasoned player in the world of dating apps and was a pioneer in utilizing algorithms to help users find matches that best aligned with what they were looking for. eHarmony gives users a "relationship questionnaire" to fill out as soon as they have created their online account. The questionnaire will help you create a personality profile that will aid in matching you with other profiles that have similar preferences to you. Thus, from the get-go, eHarmony intends to help bring profiles together with who they feel will click best with one another.

At the beginning of every day, eHarmony will recommend a flurry of profiles that best suit your preferences and provide you with information regarding both of your areas of compatibility. If both parties are interested in the profile that was suggested to them, then both parties will connect and can begin communicating with each other.

eHarmony is mainly targeted at both males and females who are looking to get married and are in search of a long-term partner. eHarmony is used to help both men and women find their Mr./Ms. Right. eHarmony has a free version, but it also has an optional premium version available for their users to subscribe to that has many added benefits. eHarmony's premium version is currently at a rate of $40–$60 a month for six months. eHarmony's premium version offers its users unlimited matches, unlimited communication, advanced search features, no ads, and access to view all photos of users who recently viewed your profile. There are many ways you can stand out on eHarmony: Be upfront and honest on your profile. Don't try to be too funny for your own good. Give yourself realistic expectations. Don't get caught up with matches that aren't interested in you (don't be clingy). Avoid overusing filters and image manipulation tactics—show your true self.

Grindr (IOS and Android)

Grindr is one of the leading dating apps for gay and bisexual men. Grindr is designed to help gay and bisexual men link up with and develop connections with other like-minded men in their area. Creating your profile on Grindr is pretty simple, as the interface of Grindr focuses primarily on uploading a couple of profile pictures, choosing a username, and answering a few simple questions so other users can get to know you a little better. Grindr has also implemented a feature known as Tribe. It helps other users find you with greater ease. Some of the tribes you can choose from on Grindr include Jock, Transexual, Twink, and Bear. Selecting a tribe makes it far easier for you to find other users that fall within your preferences, and it allows you to get chatting in minutes. Unlike apps like Tinder or Bumble, there is no swipe system, and anybody can message anybody regardless of whether they have a mutual connection or not. It is a pioneer app for the LQBTQ+ and a benchmark app that many LGBTQ+ dating apps of modern times have used as a blueprint.

Grindr is primarily targeted toward gay and bisexual men. Grindr's purpose is to help safely connect gay and bisexual men to form relationships. There is also a bit of a hookup culture attached to the app. Grindr has a free version for its users, but there are also two premium options, known as Grindr Xtra and Grindr Unlimited, that users can subscribe to for additional benefits. Grindr Xtra is currently at a rate of $20 per month, and Grindr Unlimited is currently at a rate of $50 per month. Some of the awesome features that are included with Grindr's premium versions include no ads, viewing 600 profiles at a time, access to global chat, premium filters that make your search easier, read receipts, and the ability to see who viewed your profile. Here's how you can stand out on Grindr: Start the conversation with an interesting pick-up line. Read the signs! If he isn't into you, move on. Make use of Tribes. Make your intentions clear in your profile. Lastly, make use of a face pic!

Her (IOS and Android)

Her is similar to Grindr. However, this app is particularly designed for lesbian and bisexual women. You will need to sign up using your Facebook or Instagram account and create your profile. Note that it will not post anything on your Facebook or Instagram accounts that you have used to sign up for the app. Once you sign up with either one of your social media accounts, you will be given a chance to connect with thousands of other verified Her users in and around your area. You can even connect with Her users globally. The app focuses on a system of liking other Her users' photos that they uploaded, and if the feeling is mutual, then the app will allow you and another Her user to connect and start up a conversation.

It is important to note that Her is not just about meeting new people to set up potential dates and relationships, but it is also an app that offers a flurry of social features, pressing news articles regarding the LGBTQ+ community, news on upcoming events, and many more. Her is one of the leading apps for lesbian and bisexual women (Corpuz, 2019).

Her is primarily targeted toward lesbian and bisexual women. Her's primary focus is to help safely connect gay and bisexual women to form relationships. Her has a free version for its users, but there is also a premium option that users can subscribe to for additional benefits. Her premium is currently at a rate of $14.99 per month. Some awesome features that Her premium boasts include no intrusive ads, the ability to go incognito, the ability to see who likes your profile, access to advanced features to aid in your search, the ability to rewind on profiles, unlimited swiping, read receipts, and one free boost every month. Some tips to stand out on Her include the following: not being afraid to make the first move, writing a catchy bio, being honest with your intentions, and not being overly critical.

Hey Baby (IOS)

Hey Baby is a dating app designed specifically with single parents in mind. The app realized that many single parents may not feel particularly comfortable swiping through dating sites knowing they had children. This is often due to the stigma attached to having children in the dating world, as well as the socially conditioned public perception of carrying unwanted baggage. However, Hey Baby recognized the pain point that single parents were experiencing in their search for love on the internet and thus marketed their app to be positioned for people who already have children. The app is also positioned toward people that feel strongly that they definitely want children in the future and thus helps pair people up with like-minded matches.

Hey Baby has further distinguished itself from other online dating competitors by focusing on using a fun relationship-focused questionnaire. This questionnaire is used to match profiles together based on their compatibility regarding how they answered the questionnaire. Questions relating to children and what your current family/marriage situation is like will pop up fairly early on, thus helping you match with people in a similar situation that you are in. Hey Baby's questionnaire system saves you a lot of time from swiping left or right on countless profiles as the questionnaire is designed to find somebody that aligns with your preferences from the get-go. The app is still incredibly new and still finding its feet. It is only available on Apple at the moment. However, we have a hunch that it will be a roaring success. Go check it out on IOS now!

Hey Baby is primarily targeted toward single parents. It primarily focuses on connecting like-minded single parents together to forge both romantic or friendly relationships. At the moment, Hey Baby is free for all its users and is a fantastic platform for any single parent looking for companionship. Here are tips on how you can stand out on Hey Baby: Answer the questionnaire as honestly as you can. Be true with your intentions. Upload recent pictures. And finally, don't be afraid to brag about your kids—it's pretty much the only dating app you can do that, so go ahead.

Once (IOS and Android)

Once takes a unique take on online dating by slowing down the pace of other dating apps that rely on frantic swiping. Once is designed to help you find your ideal match one profile at a time. They do this by pairing you up with one potential match every day, and then you have 24 hours (similar to Bumble) to connect before the connection is lost forever. If there is mutual reciprocation on both ends after 24 hours, you can continue to chat without time restraints. The point of Once is to move away from being bombarded with a never-ending string of profiles. Instead, they allow you to just focus on one profile at a time with the idea that you will have more time to build a stronger connection with limited distractions.

The matches that Once set you up with once a day are done through algorithms, so it learns what your preferences are from past interactions to pair you up with an ideal match for the next few days to come.

Once is primarily targeted toward male and female single millennials. It focuses on connecting its users with only one ideal match a day, thus giving you the chance to build a solid connection without any distractions from other profiles. Once offers both a free version and a premium subscription version with added benefits to their users. Once premium is currently at a rate of $19.99 per month. It boasts awesome features, such as finding out who gave your profile 4–5 stars, defining distance settings to provide you with greater accuracy for your searches, finding out whether another profile passed you or not, gaining three more matches a day, and tailor-made preferences on a permanent basis. Here's how to stand out on Once: Avoid blurry group photos. Use quality images with high resolution. Get your friends to give you some advice on your profile. Lastly, be honest with your intentions.

Plenty of Fish (IOS and Android)

Plenty of Fish is probably the biggest dating app available in terms of size. Plenty of Fish boasts an enormous number of users. In fact, they have more than 70 million users worldwide and have dipped their toes in the entire English-speaking world. This app may not have all the best features around, but it certainly makes up for it with its enormous presence and breadth around the globe.

When creating your profile with Plenty of Fish, you upload a couple of simple profile photos and stipulate your age, profession, education, and other small details about yourself. It is as easy as that. Once you have created your relatively simple profile, you will be able to scroll through potential matches and strike up a conversation with them through messages. Plenty of Fish is constantly making small tweaks to their formula, such as their "live stream" feature, which encourages video dates. It also allows you to link up your social media accounts to your Plenty of Fish profile.

Plenty of Fish is targeted toward everyone—yes, we mean everyone. The main focus of Plenty of Fish is helping users meet singles in their areas, finding a potential relationship, and helping users get to know awesome new people. Plenty of Fish offers a free version and a premium subscription version with added benefits to their users. Plenty of Fish premium is currently at a rate of $6.78–$8.35 per month. It boasts awesome added benefits. You can enjoy "read" receipts, unlock every user's extended profile, send three gifts a day, and see everybody who visited your profile. Plus, there are no ads. Here's how to stand out on Plenty of Fish: Be authentic. Be open with your intentions. Be confident. Radiate positivity. Make your interests known.

Snack (IOS)

TikTok meets Tinder—that pretty much sums up Snack. Snack is TikTok but for dating, as the app is designed to emphasize funny, cute, and appealing short videos. Once you have created your profile on Snack, you will search through a feed of videos that other users have posted and see if any of them light a spark in you. Once you have found another user's video that interests you, you need to favorite it. If they favorite one of your videos in return, then you will match and will be able to message each other.

With Snack emphasizing videos as its drawing card, it makes it a great dating app to consider using during the

COVID-19 pandemic since the world is encouraged to practice social distancing for the time being. Snack is still a new player in the dating app game and thus can only be downloaded for iPhone. However, you can sign up as an Android user, and Snack will notify you as soon as the app launches for Android. Just like Hey Baby, we believe this app will take off fast!

Snack is primarily targeted toward single male and female millennials under the age of 30. Snack focuses on connecting singles through short videos to entertain one another and form lasting relationships. At the moment, Snack is free for all its users. Here are some tips on how you can stand out on Snack: Be creative. Don't be offensive. Keep your videos short and sweet but still fun and enjoyable. Don't be stiff—loosen up in front of the camera. Lastly, remember to have fun!

Chapter 7:

The Rules and Principles of

Digital and Online Dating

With all the tips and tricks that we have learned so far, there is one thing that is missing, and that is the rules of online dating. We have constructed our own 10 commandments of dating on the internet that you will need to become familiar with and follow at all times. Do not stray off the path of these dating commandments, as they are the most important rules that one needs to follow to reap the fruit of success in the online dating world. Consider these rules as law. They will guide you to success in your search to find your match.

Rules for People Looking to Find Love Online

Looking for love online can feel overwhelming at times due to the massive scope of the modern age of dating. Sometimes it feels like a chaotic mess and can leave even the best of us riddled with anxiety. It can also leave us feeling disappointed when we aren't getting matches straight off the bat. However, we urge you to trust the process. Many people have found their current relationship partners on the internet, and the success rate of online dating is only growing. Here are some great tips if you are new to the digital dating scene or if you just need that extra bit of help to navigate your way to success to find love online.

1. Know what you want.

To really benefit from the success of digital dating, it is crucial that you know what you want and what it is you are looking for. Are you looking for a serious relationship? Perhaps some casual dating at first? Are you looking to just meet some awesome people to add to your friendship circle? Maybe you just want to hook up and participate in casual sex? Whatever it is that you are looking for, make sure you are clear about your intentions. Sometimes starting a quick journal before you commit to a dating app can help you figure out just what type of relationship you are looking for. This way, it will be easier for you to find the ideal person. By finding out just the type of person you are looking for, you become more thoughtful and selective in evaluating which profiles you will swipe left or right on. The bottom line is that it's best to only swipe right on profiles that align with your dating/relationship preference to save both you and your potential match time and effort (Gonsalves, 2014).

2. Create a profile that matches your wants.

Your profile is everything in the world of online dating. It is the defining factor that will ultimately lead to you being swiped left or right on. It determines your success in online dating. Thus, it is crucial you put a lot of thought and energy into your profile. If you are the type of person who is mainly looking for a few laughs and some fun adventures with awesome new people, then a short and witty profile will fit your personality like a glove. If you are searching for something a little more serious and a deeper connection with somebody, then write a slightly longer bio that clearly showcases who you are and what you are looking for. Include what you like, what you dislike, and what kind of person you want to attract into your life for a committed relationship. Rhonda Milrad, a relationship therapist, says that it is okay if your profile is not a one-size-fits-all and does not resonate with everybody. After all, you're not trying to garner the attention of the world; instead, you want to attract the attention of people who align with what you are looking for. Rhonda says that it is best to write a more selective and tailored bio than a generic one (Gonsalves, 2014).

3. Send lots of messages.

When we first match with somebody online, we can often be a little shy and a bit anxious to send any messages out or respond to any messages that we receive. However, to form a connection, we need to engage, and that's the truth. We need to understand that just because we send somebody a message, it doesn't mean that we want to necessarily date them. Sending an opening message (or any message) to your match is no different from saying hello to somebody sitting next to you on the bus. We urge you to just send messages to those who catch your eye or intrigue you. Feel free to respond to any message you receive that interests you. Don't be shy; get the conversation moving.

4. Don't bother with people who aren't interested in you.

Yes, we just said to send messages freely, but there is an exception. That exception is when somebody isn't interested and shows no inclination to respond to your messages. If somebody isn't responding to your first two or three messages or if they take days to respond to you, then leave them be. There are two reasons for this happening. The first reason is they haven't been active on the app in a while and haven't seen your message. Life gets busy sometimes, and they will respond to you once they log back onto the app. The second reason is they simply are not interested in forging a connection with you—in which case, it is time to move on to the next match. Unfortunately, this is a common feature of online dating, and we need to learn to respect people's time and accept rejection humbly. Just remember that there are thousands of potential reasons why they never replied to you, and 99 percent of the time, it has absolutely nothing to do with your attractiveness or value. There are plenty of other digital fish in this online ocean.

5. Write an interesting opener.

Be original when messaging somebody for the first time. "Hey" is not going to cut it. You have thousands of other people fighting for your match's attention. You need to be imaginative and think outside the box when first messaging your match. Make sure your opening message is engaging. It is suggested that you read their profile before messaging them and comment on something on their bio (Gonsalves, 2014). If their bio is a little dry, then go through their profile pictures and write something specific about one of their photos. Just make sure it is PG at first. If you still don't know what to say even after you have read their bio and scrolled through their profile pics, then ask them a question of a shared collective experience (the country you live in, a public holiday, something specific to current events) to get the conversation going. Look at chapter 2 for some more inspiration.

6. Define the relationship.

This part can be super nerve-wracking when we get it, but it is also incredibly necessary. Once you and your match have gone on a few dates and feel that you have really hit it off with each other, it is time to start having the conversation to define your relationship. No, this doesn't mean you immediately need to give yourself labels or that you have to plunge into an exclusive relationship right then and there. It just means that the two of you are speaking openly about what the future holds for each other and why you both should continue spending time with each other as the relationship progresses.

Here are some ways you could brooch the subject:

- "What kind of relationship are you looking for at the moment? Are you looking for something more casual or something more long-term?"

- "Hey, I was wondering how you see us. Do you see us together in the future?"
- "Hey, are you seeing anybody else right now, or is it just you and I?"
- "I'm really enjoying all this time we are spending together, and I have loved getting to know you. I don't know if we're at the point of putting labels on anything, but I could definitely see this turning into a relationship in the future if things remain like this. What are your thoughts on that?"

7. Be patient.

Look, we are going to be honest with you. The dating game on the internet can be brutal and rather unpredictable, but we also know how successful it can be. You need to trust the process and give it time to work its magic. Initially, you might not set up a date with your matches for the first few months, and we want to let you know that it is totally okay. It doesn't say anything about your value or attractiveness if your digital dating game is initially dry. Dating apps have become such a phenomenon in the modern age that it has developed its own whole culture, and that often means people take some time to adjust to it. On top of that, if you have been out of the dating game for a while, you may be a little rusty, and dating itself is a process that takes some time to adjust to and feel comfortable with. So keep engaging and don't get disheartened. Have fun, as that is what dating is all about (Gonsalves, 2014). Be patient, and if you feel you need to take a break from the digital and online dating scene for a while, that is okay too. When you're ready, dive back in and find your next true love in cyberspace.

The 10 Commandments of Online Dating

Online dating is a complex animal that needs to be tamed, and the modern world of dating will take you on an emotional rollercoaster. You need to take many factors into account, which have been discussed in depth throughout all the previous chapters. It is a skill that takes practice and one that needs to be mastered over time. Remember that when looking for your match, you enter a dating pool of epic proportions; thus, it is an extremely competitive environment to plunge into. Due to the highly competitive landscape of online dating, you need to do whatever it takes to stand out from the crowd. Many things have already been discussed throughout our read; however, there are still more you need to consider before starting. Below are the 10 commandments of online dating. If you follow them, you will increase your match success rate considerably. So, we will share these dating commandments with you, and if you follow them, all you need to do is sit back and wait for all the extra right swipes coming your way.

1. Say what you mean and mean what you say.

It is no secret that we as humans appreciate it when people like us; thus, sometimes it feels only natural to be tempted to turn into an effusive people-pleaser when we meet somebody on the internet whom we are attracted to. We feel the urge to throw out tons of compliments in the hope that our "new love" will reciprocate with the same passion and affection. It is fine to throw in a couple of compliments here and there, but the problem occurs when we go overboard with our compliments straight off the bat. Compliments such as "Your eyes shine brighter than the sun itself" are a little creepy, especially when you've just struck up a conversation and know nothing about your match. Dating psychologist Madeleine Mason says that giving over-the-top compliments too early on (or just in general) is a risky game plan (Petter, 2018). Mason states that when you go overboard with your compliments, one of two things can potentially go wrong. Firstly, you and your compliments might come across as inauthentic, and secondly, you may raise suspicion of desperation or even false feelings, which will only lead to further problems down the line. The bottom line is, say what you mean and mean what you say. Be honest and be yourself.

2. Thou shalt not catfish.

This should be a given, but it still needs to be said. You must not catfish or kitten fish. Catfishing implies you have created a completely fraudulent dating profile where you are posing as a completely different identity, while kitten fishing refers to lying about small minor details on your dating profile, such as your height. Kitten fishing may sound small, but it is not, and you should never do it. It's no secret that dating apps are oversaturated with catfishes and riddled with deception. These apps have enough fake posers on them; we urge that you do not add to this number of fake accounts.

A social media analytic study was conducted by a professor at the University of Oregon. The study found that men are more likely to lie on their dating profiles concerning their occupations. However, women were found to be more guilty than men of uploading either old photos from years ago or images that have been heavily manipulated through editing (Petter, 2018). The research further found that catfishers/kitten fishers will lie on their profiles to impress potential matches, thus curating a false identity that they feel others will deem attractive. Our advice to you is to make sure you are being honest about your credentials on your dating profiles. We promise you, the truth will eventually come out, and you will be made to look like a fool. Your obvious deception may cost you not only your current date but also dates in the future. You have been warned.

3. Do not start a conversation with an emoji.

Look, there are many reasons why starting a conversation with an emoji is a bad idea. Firstly, it makes it look like you have the vocabulary of a fifth-grader. We all want to be young at heart, but this isn't a good look on us. Despite making it look like we don't know how to string a sentence together, it also comes across as being lazy and that you aren't putting much of an effort into generating a meaningful connection with your match. When you match with somebody, you want sparks to fly from the heavens. Unfortunately, an eggplant or peach emoji isn't going to cut it. In fact, stay clear from peach and eggplant emojis entirely, as according to a recent study by Plenty of Fish, those are the two most disliked emojis in the online dating scene. We're going to be blunt—a lonesome emoji on its own is not going to entice your match to reply. Dating expert Madeleine Mason's advice is to try opening the conversation with a question your match can answer and follow it up with some lighthearted sentences (Petter, 2018). Remember, you want to invite a conversation, not flash your presence.

4. Do not play the waiting game.

Forget the notion that you have to wait hours before you can text back so as not to come across as desperate. Do not fall into this trap; it is a fallacy. No, we are not saying that you have to reply to every text within a 60-second time frame—of course not. Just be careful about coming across as needy. Also, avoid texting message after message when your match clearly isn't interested in responding to you. What we are saying is that we know it is tempting to play little mind games with your match when it comes to communication. However, if you play the waiting game and take too long to reply, you may create a toxic precedent for the future of your relationship, as you're obsessing over such trivial matters so early on. Madeleine Mason suggests that you should not overthink your texting habits with your beloved/match, and instead, you should adopt the same texting habits with them as you would with your best friend (Petter, 2018).

5. Always have an exit plan.

One of the downfalls of dating on the internet is that every match you get potentially runs the risk of being a very awkward first date. Often, the two of you cringe for an hour, wondering to yourselves, "Why the hell did I agree to this?" Thus, due to this common feature of first dates with an online match, you must have an exit plan prepared. There are some rules that you need to consider when planning your perfect exit strategy.

Firstly, be polite. For example, you can say, "I've had such a great time, but my Uber is waiting for me." Secondly, never tell an outrageous lie. One example is saying, "My best friend's uncle's koala fell out of the tree and their car broke down, so I need to help get it to the vet." Thirdly and most importantly, do not dine and dash. For example, "I left my wallet at home, dammit. Can I wire you the money when I get home?"

6. Ignore the advice of your friends who met their partner organically (not online).

When you're single, aren't you tired of hearing your coupled-up friends who met their partners offline with phrases such as "You'll find someone when you least expect it"? Well, the truth is your friends who found their partners offline know nothing about the complex and ruthless world of digital dating. They may as well try and teach a pig how to fly. Madeleine Mason states that many people in relationships like to think of themselves as experts when it comes to dating. However, there is more to it than simply being in a relationship to understand the complexities of dating, especially online dating. Mason says although your loved-up friends' empathetic, well-meaning advice comes from the right place, it's often insufficient and a little degrading, especially when they suggest things like what type of photos you should upload to your dating profile.

7. Play the field with caution.

The irony of dating apps is that although they are designed to help you find a lasting relationship, they are also designed to endorse a degree of polyamory due to the way the apps are set up. This is because as soon as you swipe right on one profile, there are tens of other profiles next in line waiting to see if they fit your criteria or not. Note, it is okay to keep your options open, and if multitasking is what you're into, go forth and swipe away. However, we should warn you that life can get a bit messy when you start cultivating several romantic connections at once. There are many reasons why dating can become complicated when pursuing multiple people. For instance, you will probably find yourself repeating stories because you will most likely lose track of what you have said to your multiple matches. You may send a message by accident to one of your matches that was meant for another match. You may call your match by the wrong name—this one can be fatal. Lastly and probably the most important reason, you may find it difficult to commit to your connections because of multiple distractions. Instead of having six matches at once, you really don't even have one. Madeleine Mason says that it is fine to have more than one romantic interest in the beginning. However, once you start seeing one of your multiple matches more frequently, you should prioritize that one match over the others and eventually phase out the matches you feel less connected to (Petter, 2018).

8. Read verbal and nonverbal cues.

Verbal and nonverbal cues are as important in a digital sense as they are in person when it comes to dating. We live in the age of #MeToo, so we need to be very cautious about how our match feels about physical intimacy and whether it makes them uncomfortable or not. However, reading these cues can become quite tricky online as you don't really know each other and all you have to go on is their dating profile. Sometimes we indulge in more irrational and erratic behavior online as we feel we have fewer ties to our match on the internet than we would if we were met face-to-face. Before being rash, inappropriate, or risqué in our chats, we must use our intuition when participating in matters such as intimacy on dating apps. We need to be even more cautious when we meet them in real life, and make sure we don't force ourselves onto our potential new girlfriend/boyfriend, even if it is just a kiss. Not only will unwanted physical intimacy surely lead to the connection being obliterated, but you will most likely be blocked on all platforms, and worse, you may have a court date to attend. Mason suggests that if you are unsure where your match sits on the physical and verbal intimacy spectrum, just be straightforward and ask them. She believes it is always better to be safe than sorry, and even if you may lose the facade of "playing it cool," you will at least know where both of you stand on the matter.

9. Don't play hard to get.

Forget the notion of playing hard to get. It does not work. No, we are not saying you need to be a clingy match that reeks of desperation and trust issues—of course not. You should be proactive. What this means is you simply need to pick out a few appealing points of your match that they have mentioned in their bios and work with those (UKmatch, 2015). Highlight those points you have hand-picked and use them as inspiration to write a sweet intro message. What you mustn't do is leave your match hanging for three days without saying a word and then suddenly grace them with your presence only to go AWOL for another three days. Text habits like these will get you nowhere. They certainly won't "keep them keen" despite the myth people believe that it will. It will only make them think you are uninterested and rude and that you can't even spare 60 seconds of your day to respond. Just don't do it.

10. Do not stalk the person on social media in excess.

We all know the saying "Curiosity killed the cat." Well, that saying still holds true in the world of digital and online dating. Curiosity can send people on an emotional rollercoaster, spending hours on end scrolling through their crush's social media profile. Scrolling through a social media profile is perfectly natural. We all do it. The problem occurs when curiosity turns into obsession. Scrolling through your match's social media profile may start out as an innocent inquiry. However, things can quickly turn ugly and descend into a four-hour-long deep dive into every post they have ever posted. Often people won't stop at stalking their crush's profile; they will dive deep into the profiles of old boyfriends/girlfriends, family members, and friends. Do not fall down this rabbit hole; it is creepy and very invasive. A quick look at their social media accounts is fine, especially before a first date. It will give you some basic info on them to see if they actually are who they say they are. However, keep it at that—a quick look. Madeleine Mason suggests keeping your social media detective work to a minimum, as it will save you lots of time. Refrain from indulging in creepy behavior. On top of that, it will also prevent you from building a perfect fantasy persona of your crush based on their social media portrayal, which they will almost certainly not be able to live up to in real life (Petter, 2018).

Conclusion

No man should marry
until he has studied
anatomy and dissected at
least one woman.

—Honoré de
Balzac

As the world has evolved from generation to generation, so has dating. It has transitioned from an era of being set up by friends and sourcing telephone numbers on scrap pieces of paper to an era defined by technology and the internet. In modern times, the dating world lives primarily online, and the ways of dating pre-smartphones/internet are being phased out. The days of calling your crush/boyfriend/girlfriend on a landline phone are gone, as today we do texting and video calling. The days of approaching people in line at the grocery store or asking somebody in person for their digits have been replaced with signing up to a dating app and frantically swiping either left on profiles we are not interested in or right on profiles we find appealing. Whether it is for the better or not, it is up to you to decide. However, one thing is for certain— online dating is here to stay, and it is only growing in popularity.

Dating in the modern world has become a science that we need to become familiar with and master in order to garner the success we want to achieve. We need to know how to text and use texting as a weapon in our arsenal to flirt. It is important to become familiar with different strategies and digital tactics to increase our chances of finding love online. Throughout our reading, we have been exposed to many great ways to utilize text as a way to flirt and sustain interest from our matches and crushes. We are now in a far better position to keep the conversation flowing while still maintaining a fun and flirtatious tone throughout the conversation. If you make use of the many examples and strategies that chapter 2 has to offer, you will be in a far better position to have fun, flirty, and smooth conversations with your next potential relationship.

However, texting isn't the only weapon in our arsenal, as we have also been equipped with the knowledge of how to use images to improve our success in digital and online dating. Our profile pictures are what brands us and what will differentiate us from the thousands of other profiles on dating apps. Thus, knowing how to choose dating profile pictures will definitely increase your match rate and see us reap the benefits that online dating has to offer. Thus, just like the texting strategies, it is vital that we stay true to the tips in chapter 3 to ensure we upload the perfect pictures to help us on our search for love on the internet. Remember, we need to take note of what to avoid in our profile pictures, just as we need to pay attention to what to include in them as well.

Next on the agenda is making use of video calling in our arsenal. Video calling is a great way to get to know your match on a deeper level. It also helps long-distance couples reunite regardless of the geographical boundaries that separate them. There are many benefits of utilizing video calling. It helps create a social presence, acts as a test run before a first date, and makes the other person feel more comfortable around you. Moreover, amid a pandemic, it reduces any unnecessary risk of meeting in person. Just like choosing the perfect profile pictures, video calling also has tons of rules we need to follow. When utilizing video calling with one of your matches on your first date, make sure you follow all the tips in chapter 4. These tips can save you from a very awkward first date and can also increase your chances for a follow-up video date or a date in real life. Remember, on a video date, you are on camera, so make sure you look presentable. Eliminate distractions, be creative and original, and loosen up. If you are worried about what to actually do with your match/partner on a video date, we've got your back! Remember to make use of the awesome video date ideas we have provided you in chapter 5. They are all fantastic—going on a virtual tour of a museum you are both interested in, making use of a dinner delivery roulette, or taking a fakecation to a place you both have been dying to see.

Next up is knowing which dating app to use. We know this is tricky as Android and Apple app stores are oversaturated with options. So which one do you pick? Well, pick one or two that best align with your preferences. We have helped with your research to an extent by highlighting some of the best dating apps, such as Tinder, Bumble, Her, Grindr, Hey Baby, eHarmony, and many more. These dating apps cater to a variety of different markets and preferences. Take a look at a couple and get a feel for which app works for you. There is no harm in trying an app and then deleting it. We suggest giving a couple of them a try.

Last but not least, we've learned the 10 commandments of digital and online dating. These commandments are the most important rules to follow when venturing forth in the world of digital dating. Treat them as your ultimate guide, and do not stray off the path of these commandments under any circumstances. If you do, you will get burned, and don't say we didn't warn you.

We have provided you with all the tools you need to improve your success in the world of online dating. It is now up to you to put these tips, tricks, strategies, and digital tactics into action to help you on your search for your next romantic partner. We are confident that if you put to use all that you have learned from these pages, you will find the love you are searching for on the internet. We have one small favor to ask. If you enjoyed your read and found the advice useful, please leave a review on Amazon. We wish you the best of luck in finding your next true love!

Other eBooks & Gifts You Might Love!

https://bit.ly/3Bc8RW5

With the Win Your Ex Back eBook, you will learn:☐

- Recover From a Broken Heart
- Understand What Went Wrong
- Getting in Touch Again
- Improve Communications
- The Happy Reunion
- And so much more!

This powerful eBook will provide you with a plan for everything you need to know at getting your ex back to a successful place.

It's great information on fixing your and love it will walk you, step by step, through the exact process we developed to help people get all the info they need to be a success.

#love   #romance   #dating   #free   #selfhelp
#relationships #onlinedating #digitaldating

Use Code ExBack2021 to get it free!   **Limited** downloads.

And don't forget to join Midwest2u on Facebook.

References

Abrams, A. (2019, January 30). *The psychology of modern dating.* Psychology Today. https://www.psychologytoday.com/ca/blog/n urturing-self-compassion/201901/the-psychology-modern-dating

Ask Board. (2020). *What does plenty of fish cost and is it worth upgrading?* https://www.askboard.com/relationships/what -does-plenty-of-fish-cost-and-is-it-worth-upgrading/

Bates, P. (2017, April 18). *The perfect online dating profile picture, according to research.* MUO. https://www.makeuseof.com/tag/online-dating-profile-picture-research/

Bumble. (2021). *Bumble Boost: Everything you need to know.* Bumble Buzz. https://bumble.com/the-buzz/bumble-boost

Corpuz, J. (2019, November 19). *Best dating apps.* Tom's Guide. https://www.tomsguide.com/best-picks/best-dating-apps

DMARGE. (2020, February 29). *Social media flirting: 10 rules you're probably getting very wrong.*

https://www.dmarge.com/how-to-flirt-on-social-media

Drillinger, M. (2020, June 15). *20 virtual dating plans you can actually make in self-isolation.* Greatist. https://greatist.com/connect/virtual-dating-tips

Emery, L. R. (2016, January 12). *How to stand out on Tinder.* Bustle. https://www.bustle.com/articles/134820-how-to-stand-out-on-tinder

Entenman, E. (2018, April 19). *60 flirty texts: Examples of how to flirt over text.* The Datemix. https://www.zoosk.com/date-mix/single-life/flirting/flirty-texts-examples-of-how-to-flirt-over-text/#:~:text=Flirty%20Text%20Strategy%20%232%3A%20Be,wanted%20to%20talk%20to%20you

GDI. (2016, June 2). *How online dating culture has changed the way we date.* Global Dating Insights. https://www.globaldatinginsights.com/news/online-dating-culture-changed-way-date/

Goldfarb, A. (2013, December 22). *8 ways the internet, cell phones, and social media have ruined dating.* Thought Catalog. https://thoughtcatalog.com/anna-goldfarb/2013/12/8-ways-the-internet-cell-phones-and-social-media-have-ruined-dating/

Goldfarb, A. (2014, September 25). *What dating was like before cell phones: An explainer.* MTV News. https://www.mtv.com/news/1938570/dating-before-cell-phones/

Gonsalves, K. (2014, August 23). *11 basic rules for online dating.* Mindbodygreen. https://www.mindbodygreen.com/0-14904/10-basic-rules-for-online-dating.html

Grindr. (2021). *What is Grindr XTRA?* https://help.grindr.com/hc/en-us/articles/115008879108-What-is-Grindr-XTRA-

Groner, S. (2021, January 29). *21 virtual dates you can go on in quarantine.* Glamour. https://www.glamour.com/story/virtual-dates-you-can-go-on-in-quarantine

Healthy Framework. (2021). *Tinder Cost (Updated 2021): Tinder Gold, Tinder Plus, and Boosts.* https://healthyframework.com/dating/cost/tinder/

Jarret, C. (2016, February 12). *Relationships before smartphones and dating apps.* https://cjarrettblog.wordpress.com/2016/02/12/relationships-before-smartphones-and-dating-apps/

Joho, J. (2019, February 17). *A very efficient guide to not wasting your time while online dating.* Mashable.

https://mashable.com/article/online-dating-guide-for-busy-professionals-efficient-tips/

Laurence, E., & Robinson, K. (2020, April 15). *45 flirty texts your crush won't be able to leave on read.* Seventeen. https://www.seventeen.com/love/dating-advice/g3/flirty-text-message-ideas/?slide=29

Once. (2021). Once: FAQ. https://getonce.com/en/faq

Petter, O. (2018, October 10). *The 10 commandments of online dating.* The Independent. https://www.independent.co.uk/life-style/love-sex/online-dating-rules-apps-tinder-etiquette-bumble-happn-advice-a8541806.html

PicMonkey. (2016, June 30). *4 jaw-dropping tips to make your online dating profile pic sizzle.* https://www.picmonkey.com/blog/online-dating-picture-tips-to-drop-jaws

Piñeiro, S. M. C. (2020, November 25). *If you have zero idea how to flirt effectively through text, read this.* Cosmopolitan. https://www.cosmopolitan.com/sex-love/a34719771/how-to-flirt-over-texts/

Proudfoot, J. (2020, May 11). *Dating profile: Make yours stand out with these 15 expert tips.* Marie Claire. https://www.marieclaire.co.uk/life/sex-and-relationships/15-ways-to-make-your-online-dating-profile-stand-out-from-the-pack-1-118673

Sager, B., & Taylor, A. (2021, February 5). *17 virtual date ideas to get you through social distancing.* Cosmopolitan. https://www.cosmopolitan.com/sex-love/a32173236/long-distance-date-ideas/. Cosmopolitan. https://www.cosmopolitan.com/sex-love/a32173236/long-distance-date-ideas/

Sharabi, L. (2020, September 13). *Back to the future: Is video dating here to stay?* Psychology Today. Www.psychologytoday.com. https://www.psychologytoday.com/us/blog/dating-in-the-digital-age/202009/back-the-future-is-video-dating-here-stay

Stodart, L. (2020, January 28). *The best dating sites to find a connection by this weekend.* Mashable. https://mashable.com/roundup/best-dating-sites/

Strong, R. (2020, April 7). *Try these 7 expert-approved tips for more romantic FaceTime dates.* Elite Daily. https://www.elitedaily.com/p/7-facetime-date-tips-thatll-amp-up-the-romance-22752619

UKmatch. (2015, August 7). *Top 20 unwritten rules of online dating.* https://uk.match.com/p/dating-advice/20-unwritten-rules-online-dating/

Upjokes. (2021). *The 37+ best online dating jokes.*
https://upjoke.com/online-dating-jokes

Vida Select. (2020, March 16). How to make video chat
your first "date" (expert tips for success!).
VIDA   Select.
https://www.vidaselect.com/video-chat-tips-
for-dating/

Zirby. (2020). *15 video chat first date strategies to use now.*
https://zirby.co/blog/video-chat-first-
date#tinder-to-video-calling=

Image Citations

Du Preez, P. (2019). A woman texting on her cellphone. In *Unsplash*. https://unsplash.com/photos/BjhUu6BpUZA

Dumlao, N. (2021). A man holding his phone by his face with a picture of himself. In *Unsplash*. https://unsplash.com/photos/ItsW7gT8iR0

Gios, J. (2020). A list of Motivational phrases written on planks of wood. In *Unsplash*. https://unsplash.com/photos/QB1MLXS7ncM

Hernandez, C. (2021). A man holding his child in his arms. In *Unsplash*. https://unsplash.com/photos/TMpQ5R9mbOc

Ivanova, V. (2019). A person holding a stopwatch in their hand. In *Unsplash*. https://unsplash.com/photos/p3Pj7jOYvnM

Kyed, B. (2019). A woman kissing another woman on the cheek. In *Unsplash*. https://unsplash.com/photos/P7EFJs577Xg

Nguyen, C. (2020). A dinosaur exhibit in a museum. In *Unsplash*. https://unsplash.com/photos/tXmc2mVDxJc

Österblom, T. (2019). Gay pride flags. In *Unsplash.* https://unsplash.com/photos/owiVf9bFKHM

Pexels. (2020a). A man holding flowers behind his back waiting to surprise a woman by giving them to her. In *Pexels.* https://www.pexels.com/photo/man-holding-baby-s-breath-flower-in-front-of-woman-standing-near-marble-wall-935789/

Pexels. (2020b). Chocolate cookies in a cookie jar. In *Pexels.* https://www.pexels.com/photo/photo-of-chocolate-cookies-in-jar-1476330/

Pixabay. (2020). Old telephone. In *Pixabay.* https://pixabay.com/photos/phone-old-year-built-1955-bakelite-3594206/

Pixabay. (2021). Two people at a computer screen with a heart hovering over them. In *Pixabay.* https://pixabay.com/illustrations/man-woman-love-dating-email-949058/

Unsplash. (2019). A woman meditating on a beach deck during the sunset. In *Unsplash.* https://images.unsplash.com/photo-1506126613408-eca07ce68773?ixid=MnwxMjA3fDB8MHxzZW FyY2h8Mnx8eW9nYXxlbnwwfHwwfHw%3D &ixlib=rb-1.2.1&auto=format&fit=crop&w=800&q=60

Unsplash. (2020a). A care package with lots of goodies and gifts. In *Unsplash*. https://images.unsplash.com/photo-1451443700141-5ddb6d85a8fc?ixid=MnwxMjA3fDB8MHxzZWFyY2h8Mjg5fHxnaWZ0fGVufDB8fDB8fA%3D%3D&ixlib=rb-1.2.1&auto=format&fit=crop&w=800&q=60

Unsplash. (2020b). An iPhone on a bed of grass. In *Unsplash*. https://images.unsplash.com/photo-1556800467-7b7ba9da0bf8?ixid=MnwxMjA3fDB8MHxwaG90by1wYWdlfHx8fGVufDB8fHx8&ixlib=rb-1.2.1&auto=format&fit=crop&w=1500&q=80

Unsplash. (2020c). I have a crush on You written in red neon lights. In *Unsplash*. https://images.unsplash.com/photo-1534515729281-5ddf2c470538?ixid=MnwxMjA3fDB8MHxzZWFyY2h8MXx8Y3J1c2h8ZW58MHx8MHx8&ixlib=rb-1.2.1&auto=format&fit=crop&w=800&q=60

Unsplash. (2020d). Two heart emojis and a kiss emoji on a smartphone screen. In *Unsplash*. https://images.unsplash.com/photo-1591453090456-4c83e868cf46?ixid=MnwxMjA3fDB8MHxzZWFyY2h8NXx8Y2VsbCUyMGVtb2ppfGVufDB8fDB8fA%3D%3D&ixlib=rb-1.2.1&auto=format&fit=crop&w=800&q=60

Unsplash. (2020e). Woman on a video call in a coffee shop. In *Unsplash.* https://images.unsplash.com/photo-1485217988980-11786ced9454?ixid=MnwxMjA3fDB8MHxzZWFyY2h8NTl8fG9ubGluZSUyMGRhdGluZ3xlbnwwfHwwfHw%3D&ixlib=rb-1.2.1&auto=format&fit=crop&w=800&q=60

Unsplash. (2021). A digital heart made out of code. In *Unsplash.* https://images.unsplash.com/photo-1569396116180-210c182bedb8?ixid=MnwxMjA3fDB8MHxzZWFyY2h8OXx8ZGlnaXRhbCUyMGRhdGluZ3xlbnwwfHwwfHw%3D&ixlib=rb-1.2.1&auto=format&fit=crop&w=800&q=60

Weaver, L. (2019). Man at the gym working-out. In *Unsplash.* https://unsplash.com/photos/XCkc8-_s7FA